BFI FILM

D1646058

**Rob **
SERIES EDITOR

Colin MacCabe and David Meeker
SERIES CONSULTANTS

Cinema is a fragile medium. Many of the great classic films of the past now exist, if at all, in damaged or incomplete prints. Concerned about the deterioration in the physical state of our film heritage, the National Film and Television Archive, a Division of the British Film Institute, has compiled a list of 360 key films in the history of the cinema. The long-term goal of the Archive is to build a collection of perfect showprints of these films, which will then be screened regularly at the Museum of the Moving Image in London in a year-round repertory.

BFI Film Classics is a series of books commissioned to stand alongside these titles. Authors, including film critics and scholars, film-makers, novelists, historians and those distinguished in the arts, have been invited to write on a film of their choice, drawn from the Archive's list. Each volume presents the author's own insights into the chosen film, together with a brief production history and detailed credits, notes and bibliography. The numerous illustrations have been specially made from the Archive's own prints.

With new titles published each year, the BFI Film Classics series is a unique, authoritative and highly readable guide to the great films of world cinema.

Could scarcely be improved upon ... informative, intelligent, jargon-free companions.
The Observer

Cannily but elegantly packaged BFI Classics will make for a neat addition to the most discerning shelves.
New Statesman & Society

Pépé (Jean Gabin), handcuffed behind the gates of Algiers' harbour, watches the Ville d'Oran ship sail for France

CONTENTS

. . . .

Acknowledgments

. . . .

Thanks to Ed Buscombe for commissioning this book. Thanks also to friends and colleagues who made helpful comments following presentations of a longer version of Chapter 3 in Nottingham and Birmingham, and a presentation of *Pépé le Moko* at the French Institute in London. I also wish to thank those who drew my attention to or provided relevant articles, books, videotapes and other material: Dudley Andrew, Charles Barr, Anne Boston, Sandy Flitterman-Lewis, Peter Graham, Michel Marie, Giorgio Marini, Janice Morgan, Colin McArthur, Valerie Orpen, V. F. Perkins, Alastair Phillips, Keith Reader, Gian-Luca Sergi, Steven Ungar. Special thanks to Richard Dyer for hunting down the reference to the Totó le Mokó pizzeria in Rome, to Victor Burgin for sending me the videotape of his 1993 film *Venise*, which quotes two scenes from *Pépé le Moko*, and to Peter Graham for tracking down a first edition of Ashelbé's *Pépé le Moko* at the aptly named *L'Introuvable* bookshop in Paris.

As ever, thanks to Simon Caulkin for his unconditional support.

INTRODUCTION

. . . .

In 1931, the year following the centenary of the French conquest of
Algeria, the *Exposition coloniale* was staged in Paris. It was the
culminating celebration of French colonialism. Designed to 'give the
French an awareness of their Empire', the exhibition reconstructed
habitats, and displayed folkloric dances, artefacts and merchandise, from
North and West Africa, Indochina, and other far-flung colonies. The
same year, *Pépé le Moko*, a thriller written by 'Détective Ashelbé' (a
pseudonym for Henri La Barthe – Ashelbé is an homophone for the
initials H. L. B.), was published. The book, a tale of French petty
criminals sheltering in the Casbah at Algiers, belongs to the colonialist
mentality pervasive in French culture at the time. Primarily, though, it
aimed to thrill its readers with a vicarious dive into an exotic underworld,
spiced with eroticism. Ashelbé wrote at a time when the thriller was
undergoing a spectacular boom in France. Yet, unlike his contemporary
Georges Simenon, who published his first Maigret books also in 1931, he
did not leave a great mark on French popular culture.[1] The film of *Pépé
le Moko*, on the other hand, did.

Directed by Julien Duvivier in 1936, with a prestigious technical
crew and starry cast headed by Jean Gabin, *Pépé le Moko* came out on
28 January 1937. It was a box-office and critical success[2] which on its
release was described by Jean Cocteau as a 'masterpiece' and by Graham
Greene as 'one of the most exciting and moving films I can remember
seeing'.[3] *Pépé le Moko* has since continued to fascinate. The film was
remade twice in Hollywood, as *Algiers* in 1938 and *Casbah* in 1948. There
were other echoes, tributes and parodies, from Michael Curtiz'
Casablanca (1943) to Victor Burgin's *Venise* (1993), from Warner Bros.'
Pepe le Pew cartoon series (1945) to the spoof by the great Italian comic
Totó, predictably entitled *Totó le Mokó* (1949), which now gives its name
to a Roman pizzeria. When the video of *Pépé le Moko* was commercially
released in the UK in 1993, my local video shop in central London placed
it on its 'cult film' shelf.

There have also been dissenting voices. In 1937, French critic Nino
Frank called the film a 'mixture of fakery and banality, a collection of
flimsy events and conventional characters'.[4] Recently, academic writing
has turned to issues of race and ethnicity and roundly condemned *Pépé
le Moko* for its colonialism and racism.[5] It must be said that these views

are not without foundation. The events in *Pépé le Moko* are flimsy, many characters are two-dimensional and the Casbah is – mostly – a studio set. The depiction of Algiers and its 'native' inhabitants is in turn racist and orientalist. Yet, like Graham Greene, I continue to find the film exciting and moving.

Pépé le Moko, unlike Jean Renoir's *La Grande illusion* which also appeared in 1937, is not a classic in the sense of a film which makes a great humanist statement. But it is a classic nevertheless. First of all, because it gathers many extraordinarily talented artists and technicians and brilliantly sums up the best French mainstream practice of the time. French film-making in the late 1930s reached a maturity and equilibrium, which critics have been fond of calling a 'golden age'; in this respect *Pépé le Moko* is a classic because, as T. S. Eliot put it in a different context, it represents 'the perfection of the common style'.[6] *Pépé le Moko* is also a classic because it is key to the French film noir tradition of the 1930s and set the agenda for the *policier* genre that was to flourish after the war. Last but not least, it is a classic because it stars Jean Gabin in the prime of his pre-war career and at his most handsome. Like some of the greatest Hollywood movies, *Pépé le Moko* both claims and transcends its pulp fiction material, and turns it into a powerful emotional statement on identity, desire and loss. If we cannot fail, now, to examine and criticise the colonialist ideology which permeates it, we must not let this knowledge obliterate the achievements of a great film.

THE PLOT

Pépé (Jean Gabin) is a notorious French criminal, wanted by the police, especially by Inspector Slimane (Lucas Gridoux). He is in hiding in the Casbah, the Arab quarter of Algiers, where he is safe so long as he stays there, although he yearns to return to France. He rules his small gang, composed principally of Carlos (Gabriel Gabrio), Max (Roger Legris) and Jimmy (Gaston Modot), and the benevolent figure of Grand Père, the fence (Saturnin Fabre). He is loved by women (in particular by his partner Inès [Line Noro], a gypsy), and feared and admired by all. Just after a police raid fails yet again to arrest him, he meets and falls in love with beautiful Parisian *demi-mondaine* Gaby (Mireille Balin), as she visits the Casbah with her rich friends, in search of exotic thrills. She exacerbates his nostalgia for Paris.

Pierrot (Gilbert-Gil), Pépé's protégé, is betrayed by police informer Régis (Charpin) and arrested. When Pierrot comes back to the Casbah, mortally wounded, Pépé and the gang kill Régis in retribution. Pierrot's death increases Pépé's loathing for the Casbah. Frantic, he runs towards the harbour, but is stopped in time by Inès. Gaby comes back to see him as promised, and they make love. When she fails to return the next day (having been told misleadingly by Slimane that Pépé has been arrested and killed), Pépé is distraught. He is comforted by Tania (Fréhel) who sings a nostalgic song about Paris. After violently questioning the other police informer L'Arbi (Dalio), he learns that Gaby is about to sail for France. He runs to the harbour and books a passage on the same ship and manages to get on board. Just before the ship leaves, he is caught by Slimane who has been tipped off by the jealous Inès. Pépé kills himself as the ship moves out of the harbour and Gaby, on the upper deck, dreamily gazes, unaware, at the Casbah.

....

Pépé le Moko was mostly shot in the Joinville studios near Paris. Location scenes were filmed in Algiers, Toulon, Marseilles and Sète. The film's initial title was *Nuits blanches*.

N.B. Unless specified, all subsequent references to *Pépé le Moko* are to the film.

1
....
A CLASSIC FRENCH FILM

1. Julien Duvivier and French film noir
Julien Duvivier's critical reputation has had its ups and downs, but in the 1930s he was one of the top-ranking French directors. Initially a stage actor, Duvivier trained as assistant director to Marcel L'Herbier and Louis Feuillade, among others, before directing his first film in 1919. He made seventeen silent films, but his career really took off with sound, and he became one of the leading French mainstream film-makers until his death (in a car crash induced by a heart attack) in 1967. He directed more than sixty films, many of them highly successful commercially, both before and after the war. The most notable are *David Golder* (1930), *Maria Chapdelaine* (1934), *La Bandera* (1935), *La Belle équipe* (1936), *Pépé le Moko*, *Un carnet de bal* (1937) and *La Fin du jour* (1938) in the

1930s, and the *Don Camillo* films in the 1950s.[7] Duvivier is one of those film-makers who ensured the continuity that characterises classic French cinema[8] from the coming of sound to the arrival of the New Wave. He was also remarkably cosmopolitan, working in Germany, Czechoslovakia, Britain and the US as well as France. Celebrated for his professionalism, rigorous planning and virtuoso technique, Duvivier was often compared to an American studio director. Indeed, unusually for a Frenchman, he was quite successful in Hollywood, where he directed five films before and during the war: *The Great Waltz* (1938) and *Tales of Manhattan* (1942) did particularly well at the box-office; he also made *Lydia* (1941, a remake of *Un carnet de bal*), *Flesh and Fantasy* (1943), and *The Impostor* (1944, with Jean Gabin); he also worked, uncredited, on a few other US features.

Traditional film history thinks of Duvivier as an excellent 'craftsman' and 'artisan' (or, less flatteringly, 'workhorse' and 'yeoman') rather than an auteur. In the film industry, such categorisations mattered less than reliability and results. On Duvivier's arrival in Hollywood in 1938, King Vidor praised him for his ability to work fast and economically: '*Un carnet de bal* was made in six months, cost $100,000 and was a great success in Europe. *Pépé le Moko* [...] was made for only $60,000 and yet is a work of high standard.'[9] Duvivier secured some of his success by adapting literature of proven appeal, from thrillers like *Pépé le Moko* to popular classics such as Zola's *Pot-Bouille* (filmed in 1957). Like a French Michael Curtiz, he worked in a bewildering variety of genres, from biblical epic (*Golgotha*) to thriller (*La Tête d'un homme* [1932], *Pépé le Moko*), episode film (*Un carnet de bal* and *Tales of Manhattan*) to comedy (the *Don Camillo* films). He made propaganda films, especially Catholic commissions in the silent period, and two war-time propaganda films: one in France, *Untel Père et fils* (1940), and *The Impostor* in Hollywood.

But while all this points to the identity of a 'journeyman', Duvivier's status and the absence of major studios in France meant that for most of his career he had control over his material. He took an interest in professional matters,[10] occasionally acted as producer and wrote or adapted most of his scripts. He formed creative teams which ensured him more power and continuity in the fragmented French industry – for instance with scriptwriters Charles Spaak and Henri Jeanson, set designer Jacques Krauss, and stars Harry Baur and Jean

Gabin. Like most French directors, Duvivier was in control of the *découpage* (shooting script), lighting set-ups, and editing of his films, above the technicians, however prestigious, and above the will of producers. As he said, 'I always personally decided the way a particular topic would be treated [...] I always remained in control of the films I directed.'[11] Thus, despite his eclecticism, it is not surprising to find strong themes and visual features running through Duvivier's work. In the second half of the 1930s in particular, he developed his own brand of populist melodrama with his Gabin trilogy of *La Bandera*, *La Belle équipe* and *Pépé le Moko*. What I call 'populist melodrama' is more commonly known as Poetic Realism, a key artistic sensitivity in French 1930s cinema, literature, popular music and photography.[12] Poetic Realism refers to the lyrical ('poetic') depiction of everyday situations, set in working-class or lower middle-class milieux, acting out tragic or melodramatic stories on the margins of the law. But whether we call them 'populist' or Poetic Realist, Duvivier's films of the late 1930s were central to the elaboration of the aesthetics of French film noir, itself an important influence on American film noir.[13] *Pépé le Moko* may at first sight seem less central to Poetic Realism than Carné's *Le Quai des brumes* (1938) and *Le Jour se lève* (1939), because it is removed from the French working-class urban environment. But in its dazzling black-and-white visual poetry and in its pessimistic tone, including nostalgia for a lost world of the French working classes, it is a founding keystone of French noir cinema. Four features of Duvivier's work are key to this aesthetic: an expressionist use of *mise-en-scène* in its interaction of lighting, performance and décor, the depiction of popular criminal milieux, a deep-rooted pessimism, and a penchant for 'men's stories'.[14] These all found a particularly felicitous terrain in *Pépé le Moko*, as we will see.

. . . .

Pépé le Moko offers an anthology of camera angles and movements, editing, lighting and music then in use in the best of the French cinema, as well as of Duvivier's virtuosity.[15]

The novel opens with petty crook Carlo ('Carlos' in the film) hiding in Marseilles *chez* Pépé's mother, Ninette. Carlo escapes to Algiers and takes us into the Casbah to meet Pépé. The film, on the other hand, begins with a map of the Casbah and remains in Algiers until the end, moving back and forth between the Casbah and the modern town

Images from the Casbah: the map, 'strange' street
names, 'all sorts' of women

(the police headquarters and the Hotel Aletti). The camera pulls back from the map to reveal a room in the police headquarters in Algiers; the exotic location is signalled by half-lowered venetian blinds, silhouetted palm trees outside the windows and a couple of inspectors fanning themselves with their hats. As the policemen of Algiers explain to their visiting Parisian colleagues the reasons for the continued failure to capture Pépé, the dialogue establishes both his status as *caïd* (chief) and the centrality of the Casbah, his hideout. A 'documentary' montage then depicts the Casbah, before moving on to the 'fictional' Casbah. The progression from map to documentary to story reveals both the film's desire to anchor itself in the real, and its trajectory towards fantasy.

Coded as documentary with location shots, rapid editing and Inspector Meunier's authoritative voice-over, the montage (which lasts just under two minutes) shows off Duvivier's virtuosity and acts as a matrix of thematic and visual motifs for the rest of the film. The first image, a sweeping panoramic long shot of the Casbah from the top of the hill down to the harbour, encapsulates Pépé's desired journey as well as his fate. This is followed by a very fast montage of short takes (on average less than three seconds each), the camera moving from overhead shots to views down narrow alleyways, to close-ups of faces, to blurred low-angle hand-held shots which simulate the position of a person caught in the bustle of Casbah streetlife. The theme of entrapment, which began with the map showing the Casbah as enclosed fortress (the original meaning of 'Casbah') and labyrinth, is fleshed out in the montage and will be pursued across the film: we see confined, dark spaces, bars on windows and arches across streets, sinuous alleyways (the camera movement espousing their shapes), crowded cafés, a maze of split-level homes and terraces and an abundance of stairs. This is reinforced by the commentary, sprinkled with expressions such as 'tortuous and dark streets', 'tiny trap-like streets', 'holes', 'ant-hill', 'tight labyrinth'. The montage establishes straight away the colonialist notion of the Casbah as starkly alien to the Parisian inspectors and, by extension, to the viewers. Some street names picked out by the camera are simply declared exotic by the commentary ('rue de la Ville de Soum Soum'), while some link to the story to come: 'rue de l'homme à la perle' anticipates Pépé's very first appearance, holding a pearl in his hand, and his connection with Gaby and jewels; 'rue de l'impuissance,' his blocked future. The sequence ends on another major colonialist theme, the identity of the Casbah as feminine and sexual, a feminine sexuality marked as illicit since it is identified with prostitution: 'girls from all countries, in all sorts of shapes'. This in turn foreshadows the larger prostitution sub-text of the film: Pépé's discreet coding as pimp, Gaby's identity as high-class prostitute. The camera and voice-over's derogatory insistence on old, fat prostitutes will be echoed in Tania and Mère Tarte.

The novelist Italo Calvino said: 'Having seen the Casbah of *Pépé le Moko*, I began to look at the staircases of our own old city with a different eye [...]. The French cinema was heavy with odors whereas the American cinema smelled of Palmolive.'[16] The *evocative* quality of the Casbah in *Pépé le Moko* raises questions about the orientalism of the film which will be examined in Chapter 3; but it is also an index of the strong presence and *materiality* of the film's décor. The sets built in the Joinville studios for *Pépé le Moko* were extensive and spectacular, and the decision to go for a reconstruction on such a scale, even if in part due to contingencies,[17] was unsurprising for the time. René Clair's *Sous les toits de Paris* (1930) inaugurated a 'French school' of set design for the sound cinema, led by émigré designers Lazare Meerson and Alexandre Trauner who both taught or influenced other practitioners, among them *Pépé le Moko*'s designer, Jacques Krauss. The characteristic quality of this school was its combination of painstaking fidelity to real cityscapes (usually Paris) with subtle, poetic abstraction. While the use of sets was largely dictated by sound technology, the French school turned them into an aesthetic tool. Many fervently defended the superiority of sets over location. Léon Barsacq (who designed the sets for Renoir's *La Marseillaise* and Duvivier's *Pot-Bouille* among others) even argued that '[t]he decor of *Pépé le Moko*, which reproduces Algiers' Casbah, has an evocative power that location shooting does not possess', because the real location would 'dissipate the viewer's interest with its involuntary picturesqueness'.[18]

Duvivier, in fact, was familiar with North African locations, as he had shot large sections of *Les Cinq gentlemen maudits* (1931) in Morocco and *La Bandera* in the Sahara. But these are adventure films calling for outdoor scenes, the first with depictions of religious ceremonies and the estate of colonialist Harry Baur, the second with the portrayal of legionnaires' lives. Duvivier inserted some location views of the Casbah in *Pépé le Moko* beyond the opening montage. In the scene that follows

Pépé's first encounter with Gaby, in which he gazes at the sea and Inès puts her laundry out to dry, the switch from the establishing location shot to the closer studio shot is evident, as it is in the later scene on the terrace of the Hotel Aletti. This takes in the harbour (location), and moves on, following Slimane, into a studio shot of Gaby and her friends at table. These location moments are brief, though. Sets fitted better an urban topic like *Pépé le Moko* and the majority of the Casbah views were recreated in the Joinville studios. Jacques Krauss was used to working with Duvivier, having designed the sets of *Le Paquebot Tenacity* (1933), *Maria Chapdelaine*, *La Bandera* and *La Belle équipe*. Trained as a painter, he reproduced the look of the Casbah streets with a meticulousness and, despite Barsacq's assertion, a love of picturesque detail borne out by a comparison with contemporary postcards (bearing in mind the self-selectivity of these postcards, designed for tourists). While providing local colour, the sets facilitated the highly controlled interaction between décor, camera and characters that distinguishes the best of French cinema of the time and which Duvivier's fluid camerawork brilliantly exemplifies. A scene early on in the film, in which Pépé and Slimane take a walk, throws into relief this tight triangular relationship.

The scene begins outside Inès' front door, where Pépé and Slimane humorously discuss Pépé's sex-appeal, while Pépé's acolytes Max and Jimmy silently watch (these two will not utter a word during the whole film). Their conversation is covered in one take of 25 seconds from a high angle medium-long shot. They move on, and the camera, from a reverse low angle position, picks up Pépé and Slimane on the stairs at the top of a steeply inclined street. They move down the street, at a leisurely pace, preceded by the back-tracking camera, as Pépé greets people standing by the side of the street. The two men pause by a house corner on the left. They resume walking and then pause a second time, as Pépé eats a kebab from a stall, he and Slimane framed by an overhead arch. Max and Jimmy continue to shadow Pépé: Jimmy plays with his *bilboquet* (cup-and-ball) to the right, Max stands smiling to the left. A string of peppers spans the arch diagonally, adding depth of field. They resume their walk, the camera preceding them again, and pause a third time to the right, to let a flock of sheep move up the street. Pépé eats something (a cake?) from a stall to the right. After the frantic montage described earlier, and the night-time police raid (analysed later), the function of this scene is to display the 'ordinary' bustle of the Casbah, with people and animals milling around, and Pépé's easy relationship with Slimane. Throughout the scene, the camera is mobile, imitating a passer-by and intensifying the movement of the street, as people move in the opposite direction. The scene also testifies to the literal and metaphorical closeness between Pépé and the Casbah. He addresses people and they repeat his name, like an incantation. He touches them on his way down. The design and positioning of the walls and arches tightly encase him. The three pauses show this closeness in more detail: Pépé touches the walls, slaps the hand of a stallholder, prods Slimane. He is in touch with, and at home in, the Casbah. As we will see in Chapter 4, the remake *Algiers*, though reputed to be a carbon copy of *Pépé le Moko*, establishes a greater distance between décor and characters. The French tradition epitomised by Duvivier makes the décor, more centrally, an actor in the drama.

The scene described above, lasting over two minutes, is made up of only five takes, four of them lasting 25 seconds or more and including camera movements. Although exceptionally long, they are indicative of Duvivier's general tendency, like most of his French colleagues, to use longer takes than in Hollywood (on average 10 seconds as opposed to 5 to 7 in American cinema).[19] But as this scene shows, Duvivier's long takes are not the static ones found in the 'filmed theatre' pieces of Marcel Pagnol and Sacha Guitry. The scene is typical of his dynamic camerawork, and its ability to create a tight bond between characters and their environment. At the same time Duvivier's camerawork differs from the idiosyncratic style of Jean Renoir and his occasionally dizzy camera movements; for instance, his celebrated 360° pan-shot in *Le Crime de Monsieur Lange* (1935). At times breathtakingly elegant and even flashy, Duvivier's camera movements are nevertheless on the whole smooth, justified by the action and motivated by the actors' movements, and thus often invisible. Two examples. One is the scene in which Pépé 'explodes' with anger and frustration at Chani's café, an archetypal moment in the Gabin performance. The climax of the scene is covered in one 45 seconds-long take, with four slight reframings. The other is the scene towards the end of the film when Pépé interrogates and punishes L'Arbi, which achieves a similar although more spectacular effect. Again, the climax of the scene is dealt with in one 2-minute-long mobile take subordinated to Gabin's movements as he increases his pressure on

L'Arbi to tell the truth. The combination of filming in real time, of Gabin's body language which exudes repressed violence, and the tightness of the framing and movement of the camera following him produce an extraordinary tension as well as a 'reality effect' which anchors the spectator's identification. This contrasts with moments of distanced spectacle, such as Gabin's singing or his descent to the harbour against obvious backdrops.

Together with the long and mobile takes described above, Duvivier uses short takes, often at a slant, to highlight details of the Casbah or of characters' faces. Extreme camera angles are seen throughout the film: peering down into a narrow street, looking up steep stairs to greet Pépé's legs, pointing down into Grand Père's house. Slanted shots of faces isolate them from their surroundings and turn them into distanced and 'strange' icons. This is often true of the faces of Arab characters such as Slimane, or the young woman who shelters Gaby. By contrast, the exchange of close-ups between Pépé and Gaby during their first meeting follows a more classic shot/counter-shot alternation. The emphasis on iconic faces also occurs in scenes where tension builds up, notably during the punishment of Régis, when the camera cuts away rapidly with multiple shots of the menacing or sardonic faces of Pépé's acolytes, and of Régis' increasingly terrorised expression, to the rhythm of the pianola which Régis unwittingly sets off as he falls on to it. This 'expressionist' use of the camera contributes to a disorientating effect, characteristic of film noir.

The other, more obvious, aspect of Duvivier's *mise-en-scène* which belongs to the noir aesthetics is his use of lighting and, in particular, chiaroscuro. In this respect, *Pépé le Moko* allows us to see the French film noir of the late 1930s as the 'missing link' between Germany in the 1920s and Hollywood in the 1940s. German cinema was held in high regard in France, and frequent journeys took place between Berlin and Paris, including those by Duvivier. This close rapport is epitomised in the title of his third sound film, *Allo Berlin?... Ici Paris!* (1931), a bilingual romance between two telephone operators (a French woman and a German man). French cinematographers were strongly influenced by their German colleagues, some of whom, like Kurt Courant and Eugen Schüfftan, worked in France in the 1930s. *Pépé le Moko*'s Jules Kruger and Marc Fossard were no exceptions. Duvivier's 1935 *La Bandera* already offered the archetypal noir visual motif of

Noir lighting: Régis (Charpin, left) and Aïcha (Olga Lord) outside the Ali Baba café

Noir lighting: Gaby (Mireille Balin, left) and Slimane (Lucas Gridoux) at the Hotel Aletti

venetian blinds throwing black and white shadows over Gabin's face. *Pépé le Moko* returns to this motif several times: for example, when Régis and Pierrot read the fake 'mother's' letter, when Gaby wipes Maxime's forehead at the hotel, and when Slimane talks to Gaby in the hotel lobby. The striped shadows link characters with décor, enveloping them in an atmosphere at once exotic and menacing. Other signs of exoticism such as silhouetted palms, ironwork, carved columns are frequently included in these shots.

Although these are theoretically daytime scenes, the overall effect is of darkness. Duvivier, Kruger and Fossard throughout the film imaginatively exploit the Casbah décor to create lighting patterns. For instance, when Pépé and Gaby come out in Mère Tarte's courtyard after they have made love, light shining through a central well strongly illuminates faces from below. The effect is unrealistic in terms of time and location, but it prolongs the mood of erotic glamour of the previous scene. When Inès looks from the street into the Ali Baba café, in which Pépé, Gaby and Slimane are gathered, the combination of lighting and of the lacy curtain superimposes an intricate 'oriental' pattern over the image, emphasised by the window frame. The reverse shot of Inès' face, heavily criss-crossed by shadows, together with her 'gypsy' look (large ear-rings, darkened skin and hair), evokes a mood of alienation beyond the meaning of her character at this particular point. In indoor scenes, visible light sources create intense pools of light in the surrounding darkness, for instance at Grand Père's, when the gang discusses their latest burglary, and later when Aïcha comes to say that Pierrot has disappeared, as well as during Régis' interrogation. The latter begins in the dark, with Pépé and Régis as dark silhouettes, until Pépé switches on a lamp (a globe held by a tiny figure). Close examination shows that supplementary spotlights from other angles discreetly enhance the glow on characters' faces, eyes and hair, but the use of a dramatically visible light source is highly effective in bestowing a mood of danger and mystery, even to the most ordinary room, and in aestheticising the criminals.

Nowhere is this more in evidence than with Pépé, because of the special relationship between Gabin and the camera. With *La Bandera* and *La Belle équipe*, but more intensively in *Pépé le Moko*, Duvivier refined a way of lighting Gabin's face in close-up. Fully exploiting the star's minimalist acting in close-ups, Duvivier used spotlights to throw thin bands of light on his hair, creating a permanent shine, and on his eyes. As Gabin had pale eyes, the effect introduces a softness and vulnerability in his otherwise rugged face with its irregular nose and sharply defined jaw and mouth. We see a 'soft' version of this in the first shot of Pépé's face, as the camera tracks up from his hand holding a pearl, and in the first meeting with Gaby; and a 'hard' version during the first card game, in the back room at Chani's. Gabin turns his head to speak to Pierrot, looking up towards the camera. His eyes are sharply illuminated, to such a degree that, legend has it that he suffered burns. The effect on screen is to signal him as vulnerable and as 'other'. The lighting detaches him from his mundane card game, lifts him from vulgar hoodlum to tragic hero. Duvivier's *mise-en-scène*, especially in *Pépé le Moko*, must thus be credited with perfecting Gabin's 'tragic' persona, a persona which will then be pursued with similar techniques by Jean Grémillon in *Gueule d'amour* (1937), Jean Renoir in *La Bête humaine* (1938) and Marcel Carné in *Le Quai des brumes* and *Le Jour se lève*.

From the evocation of the Casbah streets to the hero's state of mind, *Pépé le Moko* deploys a web of glamorous noir images which elevate its basic story of petty hoodlums, incompetent policemen and kept woman into the realm of poetry. But the effect is not only visual. In 1937, French cinema was a talking, singing and dancing cinema. The spectator's experience of *Pépé le Moko*, with its intricate musical score and memorable dialogue, is also very much an oral one.

Duvivier perfected special lighting for Gabin's face

2. A cinema of words and music

The coming of sound cinema propelled the French language to the fore, turning it into a mark of national distinction. Though it was an impediment to export, language brought other benefits, in particular the use of literary and theatrical texts and the inclusion of songs. This move renewed the popularity of French cinema at its own box-office, but sparked off a huge critical debate about the pros and cons of 'filmed theatre'. Language and songs, however, forged the identity of French cinema, anchoring it overtly in earlier traditions. In *Pépé le Moko*, this is a particularly complex issue, as the linguistic marks of national identity attached to many of the characters are, by the same token, the marks of exclusion of others, an issue we will return to in Chapter 3.

Language entailed a new aesthetic. French cinema became an especially dialogue-driven cinema and the 1930s saw the ascent – in terms of adaptations and of dialogue registers – of the *boulevard* tradition, marked by social derision and witticism. Compared to its American or British equivalents (Noël Coward, Oscar Wilde), the French *boulevard* theatre offered a greater mix of language registers and thus, up to a point, could include popular vernacular and slang. This particular theatrical tradition also importantly informed films not based on plays and which otherwise belonged to populist genres, such as *Pépé le Moko*. The importance of dialogue for French cinema is shown by the creation of the category of *dialoguiste*, a dialogue writer often (although not always) separate from the scriptwriter. The credits of *Pépé le Moko* are in this respect typical. Duvivier was in charge of the script with Ashelbé, with help for the adaptation (Jacques Constant), but the dialogue was written by Henri Jeanson. The latter, a journalist for the satirical weekly *Le Canard enchaîné* and a famous wit, was, with poet Jacques Prévert, the most famous *dialoguiste* of classic French cinema. Their *bons mots* became part of popular French culture – for example, Prévert's 'bizarre, bizarre' in *Drôle de drame* (1936), and Jeanson's 'atmosphère, atmosphère' in *Hôtel du Nord* (1938). Jeanson's dialogue for *Pépé le Moko* is testimony to his craft, peppered with linguistic gems absent from Ashelbé's novel, whose full flavour is, alas, untranslatable. For instance, Régis talking about Pierrot: 'C'est un mauvais garçon, mais un bon fils' (he's a bad boy but a good son), puns on the multiple meaning of the word *garçon* as boy, son and hoodlum. Pépé's remark to Slimane that 'avoir l'air d'un faux-jeton à ce point-là, j'te jure que c'est vraiment de la franchise!' (to look so false is a form of honesty) is also typical in its mixture of sophisticated wit and slang. Throughout *Pépé le Moko*, the dialogue conveys the criminal and popular milieu of the film, but it also addresses the audience directly, above the head of the characters as it were, demanding to be savoured for its own sake. Sentences call attention to themselves, to be noticed and remembered, and indeed they are.

Jeanson's most famous creation (also not in the book) is the scene where Gaby and Pépé dreamily exchange street names after they discover they are both from Paris, coinciding on 'la place Blanche!' The scene is a brilliant condensation of the touristic appeal of Paris with precise social topography, which moreover reflects the stars' images. Gaby's itinerary is that of luxury shopping and commodified entertainment: it starts at the Champs-Elysées and takes in Opéra, boulevard des Capucines, rue Montmartre and rue Fontaine to end up at place Blanche, while Pépé reaches the same destination via working-class rue Saint-Martin, Gare du Nord, Barbès, La Chapelle, and boulevard Rochechouart. Place Blanche is the meeting point of working-class and criminal Montmartre with seedy night-club land Pigalle. In Francis Carco's populist novel *Jésus la Caille* (1914), pimps, prostitutes, housewives and bourgeois on a night out also mingle in place Blanche, brought together by entertainment. For on place Blanche stands the Moulin Rouge, one of the most famous Parisian music-halls, opened in 1889. Though not actually mentioned in this particular exchange, the Moulin Rouge acts as a mythical reference point for Gaby and Pépé, connecting them with the French *café-concert* and music-hall traditions explicitly represented in *Pépé le Moko* by Gabin's and Fréhel's songs, to which we will now turn.

Gabin's 'Pour être heureux dans la vie', which occurs an hour into the film, is a rhythmic rumba by the film's composer Vincent Scotto. It is typical of the joyful tunes of the time, many of them produced by Scotto. Although the happy music and lyrics about all-important love reflect Pépé's happiness (this is the morning after he has made love to Gaby), the song is otherwise at odds with the pessimistic mood of the film. It makes sense however as a testimony to the importance of song in French popular culture, and the close links that developed between sound cinema and the music business. Printed song-sheets, radio and records advertised the film, and vice versa. Today, innumerable vinyl

Tania (Fréhel) sings her nostalgic song. Top: hand-cranking the gramophone; middle:
picture of the young Fréhel; bottom: the older Fréhel sings over her own recorded voice

and CD compilations – of Gabin, Fréhel and French *chanson* – perpetuate the memory of *Pépé le Moko*'s songs. 'Pour être heureux dans la vie' is also an allusion to Gabin's early career on the music-hall stage, singing just this kind of song. Duvivier illustrates the performance of the song in a way which evokes both the tradition of live spectacle and the cinema audience. We see relatively little of Gabin himself, only a few long shots of him on Inès' terrace, and his reflection in a mirror. Instead, Duvivier offers a fast montage of Pépé's audience which recalls the opening montage depicting the Casbah. We see in rapid succession a range of Casbah inhabitants: an old woman sifting grain, a young woman de-lousing her son, prostitutes, a young girl also sifting grain, a (male) shoe mender beating a shoe to the rhythm of the music, women dancing likewise to the rhythm of the song. An expression of Pépé's state of mind, the song acts to blend a community of spectators, some of whom, like the shoe-mender, even incorporate its rhythm into their bodies. The song performs the ideological operation of bonding the Casbah to the French performer and through him the film's spectator.

Fréhel's song, on the other hand, operates on a more abstract level. Performed on screen only to Pépé, it addresses directly the film's spectator. Fréhel's 'Où est-il donc?' is a slow ballad, also composed by Scotto, though predating the film. It is inserted in the film more as a 'quote' than Gabin's song. Tania plays a marginal character in the film and Fréhel's cultural identity was that of a singer, not an actress. One of the great exponents of *chanson réaliste*, Fréhel had a double career. She was a young and very beautiful singer in pre-First World War *café-concert*, described by Colette in her 1911 novel *La Vagabonde*. She left France because of personal misfortunes (including a broken affair with Maurice Chevalier). An older, fatter and altogether more tragic Fréhel made a come-back in the 1920s and had a modest film career in the 1930s, usually in singing cameos. Her more important roles, apart from *Pépé le Moko*, are in Anatole Litvak's *Coeur de Lilas* (1931, also with Gabin), Sacha Guitry's *Le Roman d'un tricheur* (1936), Pierre Chenal's *La Maison du Maltais* (1938) and Albert Valentin's *L'Entraîneuse* (1938). Her identity in her second career added layers of nostalgia for her lost youth and glamour to her melodramatic personal life. The elegiac words of 'Où est-il donc?', ostensibly about a vanishing Paris, are also about her earlier career, familiar to the 1937 spectator. This double nostalgia is visualised by Duvivier in the image of her hand cranking up the old phonograph as well as a picture of the young Fréhel on the wall behind her. The self-referential nature of Fréhel's song is illustrated furthermore by the fact that it has no equivalent in the remakes *Algiers* and *Casbah*, whereas Pépé's song has (see Chapter 4). However, on a deeper level, Fréhel's song is strongly linked to the major theme of Pépé's nostalgic desire for Paris, and forms part of a network of references that runs through the film. The lyrics speak of the 'Moulin [Rouge] de la place Blanche' where Pépé and Gaby symbolically meet, and of 'mon bistrot du coin' (my local café), echoing Pépé's declaration to Gaby that she reminds him of 'cups of *café-crème* at the café terrace'. As Fréhel sings the words 'thinking of Paris', a medium shot of Gabin lying down provides the only cut in the sequence which is otherwise covered in two long static takes of her face. The choice of lengthy and static takes intensifies the emotional power of Fréhel's voice and of the song's lyrics, and is in keeping with its slow pessimism. Duvivier, who had used another *chanteuse*, Damia, in *La Tête d'un homme*, understood these singers' emotional power, as did Cocteau who wrote: 'Fréhel, who risked slowing down the action [of the film] with a "number", is incredibly moving.'[20]

As well as the two songs, Vincent Scotto (who was of Napolitan origin) wrote most of the music heard in *Pépé le Moko*. A composer of operettas, of over 4,000 songs and of musical scores for 200 films, Scotto was one of the pillars of French twentieth-century popular music. His range was as wide as his production was formidable, from pessimistic *chanson réaliste* to the rumba. Among his best-known hits are 'J'ai deux amours' (Josephine Baker), 'Prosper' (Maurice Chevalier) and 'Marinella' (Tino Rossi). He worked for many French directors, including Pagnol, for whom he also appeared as an actor in *Jofroi* (1934). Scotto also composed one of the classics of the *chanson coloniale*, 'Ma petite tonkinoise', sung, among others, by Josephine Baker. *Pépé le Moko* is thus a good compendium of both Scotto's talent and of the range of French popular music of the time. It includes the two songs described above, and an extensive score which covers most scenes. Two main themes can be heard: an elegiac 'Western' tune which relates to Pépé, especially his attempts to leave the Casbah and his relationship to Gaby; and orientalist pastiche, for example over the police raid. This meshes with genuine Arab music, the work of composer Mohamed Yguerbouchen, heard over Casbah street scenes. But Yguerbouchen's music provides mostly local colour, and the dominance of French popular music is in no doubt. Apart from the two songs performed by Gabin and Fréhel, and Scotto's extensive score, two instances further limit the oral space allocated to indigenous music. The first occurs as Gaby and Pépé meet for the second time, in the Ali Baba café. Gaby's friends put on a record of indigenous music because 'it must be amusing', but soon replace it with a fox-trot which 'will be more fun'. Although Gaby's friends are signified to the spectator as faintly ridiculous, the result is still that Pépé and Gaby dance to Western music. The second instance is after Pierrot's death, when Pépé berates his friends, especially Jimmy, who had put on a record of Arab music, and says: 'I'm fed up. I've had enough of their music, of their gibberish,' prompting Jimmy to quickly take the record off the gramophone. Here again, although Pépé's behaviour at this point is shown to be excessive, the effect is to connote the indigenous music as a nuisance and to silence it.

3. Performance

The centrality of dialogue and songs in *Pépé le Moko*, as in French 1930s cinema as a whole, went hand in hand with the pre-eminent role of actors. In the popular cinema of the 1930s, two strands emerged. On the one hand were the stars, who tended towards the understated/naturalistic (Gabin) and the glamorous/ethereal (Balin). On the other hand was an array of actors in secondary roles, delineating a social typology through physique, voice, diction and accent. Dubbed the 'eccentrics' of French cinema, in Raymond Chirat's phrase,[21] they were no mere character actors. The 'eccentrics' formed a dense population of familiar and much-loved faces and voices whose resonance with French audiences, as well as in French film historiography, is far higher than their film roles (there is even a CD compilation of 'eccentrics' songs'). In *Pépé le Moko*, the most prominent of these 'eccentrics' are Charpin, Saturnin Fabre and Gaston Modot; Dalio, who became an important 'eccentric', was here at the very beginning of his film career. Charpin plays Régis, the slimy police informer. His southern bonhomie, familiar from the Pagnol trilogy of *Marius* (1931), *Fanny* (1932) and *César* (1936) (referenced in the *belote* card game), is used counter-typically to achieve a sinister portrait, underlined by his constant sweating. Saturnin Fabre (Grand Père) uses to the full his well-known droll and camp elocution. Most of the others, especially Gabriel Gabrio (Carlos), Gaston Modot (Jimmy), Line Noro (Inès), Charles Granval (Maxime), Lucas

Gridoux (Slimane) and Jean Temerson (Gravère), were actors with substantial reputations from stage and film who would often be seen in more important parts; Granval, for instance, was Monsieur Lestingois in Renoir's *Boudu sauvé des eaux* (1931), and Modot the hero of Buñuel's *L'Age d'or* (1930). As a group, the 'eccentrics' enhanced the aura of quality of the film. Individually, their image projected far beyond the part itself. In some cases, for instance Gaston Modot's silent Jimmy, it *is* the part. Nino Frank's criticism that many of *Pépé le Moko*'s characters are 'flimsy' is true on paper but not on the screen, as actors like Modot, Charpin and Fabre flesh them out through their accumulated image. These actors, who all came from the stage, are unashamedly theatrical in their gestures and vocal flourishes, perfect for Jeanson's outrageously over-written lines. Paradoxically though, they also bring a sociological depth to the most clichéd characters. The 'eccentrics' had another function: their hyper-performative style is a shrine to the effortlessly understated presence of the star, Jean Gabin, and to the glamour of the couple he forms with Mireille Balin.

4. Gabin le Moko

In the typology of stars proposed by Richard Dyer,[22] Gabin in *Pépé le Moko* is a case of a near-perfect 'fit' between star image and character. Ashelbé's book was written just before Gabin started his film career, yet the part, as written, seems uncannily made for him. By the time he shot *Pépé le Moko* , his star image was formed, and the character was adapted for an even better match. The jewel in the crown of the film's creative team, Gabin is arguably as much *Pépé le Moko*'s auteur as Duvivier is.

Gabin came from the music-hall and started his cinema career in a film version of a comic vaudeville play, *Chacun sa chance* (1930). From the beginning he worked in populist cinema, but in a comic mode, in films such as *Les Gaietés de l'escadron* (1932) and *Zouzou* (1934). Concurrently, he appeared in dramatic roles, often as a petty crook, notably in *Paris-Béguin* and *Coeur de Lilas* (both 1931). For a few years he oscillated between comedy and drama. In 1935 Duvivier's *La Bandera* definitely fixed his image in the melodramatic register, and the up-and-coming actor became an overnight star. He remained the leading male star in France until the war (when he went to Hollywood), with Duvivier's *La Belle équipe*, Renoir's *Les Bas-fonds* (1936), *La Grande illusion* and *La Bête humaine*, Grémillon's *Gueule d'amour* and Carné's *Le Quai des brumes* and *Le Jour se lève*. This glorious series of classics established him as the star of both auteur and popular cinema. *La Bandera*, which, like *Pépé le Moko*, had a colonial setting, set the dual core of the Gabin image: regular working-class guy and criminal or gangster. Gabin, in short, was a 'good-bad boy': sometimes an ordinary worker driven to crime (*La Belle équipe*, *Gueule d'amour*, *Le Jour se lève*) and sometimes an outlaw who is honest at heart (*La Bandera*, *Les Bas-fonds*, *Pépé le Moko*). Gabin's charisma endowed the worker-criminal double persona with glamour and romanticism, and his performance style gave his characters both density and authenticity, even in the case of a pulp-fiction hero such as Pépé.

From the very beginning, authenticity emerged as the key attribute of Gabin's acting and reviews of his performances from the start stressed him as 'genuine'. There were two main reasons for this: his acting style, and its perceived similarity to his real life. Gabin quickly unlearned the exaggeration of the stage. Compared to the 'eccentrics' surrounding him, his speech is naturalistic, his gestures restrained and precise. His voice has the accent and intonation of the Parisian *faubourgs*, his body and walk are coded as exuding working-class solidity. His facial expressions, magnified by close-ups and lighting, are understated. Where the 'eccentrics' act for the spectator in the back row, Gabin acts for the camera. This allowed Gabin to become the emblem of an 'ordinary' yet self-contained and powerful masculinity which carries the hint of its own violence without having to show it, except in occasional outbursts. A tenacious legend that Gabin insisted on having one such outburst of anger written in all his film contracts turns out to be just that, a legend. However, these 'explosions' were common in his films and expected by the spectators. They therefore acted as moments of mini-spectacle in their own right. Though Gabin's parents were actually stage actors, publicity quickly picked up on other aspects of his upbringing which seemed better matched to his parts, and which he himself was keen to promote: his childhood on his grand-parents' farm in Mériel, north of Paris (where the Gabin museum now is located), his familiarity with the working-class areas of Paris. Carné is typical of how successfully this image-making worked when he wrote, in 1933, 'He kept from his adolescent and young man's frequentations a pronounced taste for people on the margins and for picturesque slang.'[23]

A comparison between Ashelbé's and Duvivier's Pépé reveals the film-makers' desire to conform to Gabin's image. As already mentioned,

Pépé's singing in *Pépé le Moko* is a direct reference to his stage and film career and, needless to say, it does not appear in the book. Through Gabin, *Pépé le Moko* transforms Pépé from a prosaic hoodlum-in-hiding to the towering prince of the Casbah, and from a rather nasty petty criminal to a sympathetic 'good-bad boy'. His first appearance condenses the difference between book and film. In the novel, his friend Carlo, on arrival in Algiers 'could not believe his eyes when he saw the reality of what he had imagined. What! this was the *caïd*, the Pépé whose situation was supposed to be that of a pacha. [...] He was a pariah like so many others', who, moreover, weeps while reading his mother's letter, much to Carlo's contempt. In the film, after his hallowed status has been built up by the dialogue between the policemen, we hear his voice imagining his hand as 'an oyster shell', before discovering his face enhanced by glowing lights. The adaptation keeps the basic narrative trajectory of the character, his meeting with Gaby and his death as he tries to take the boat to France. But it erases the early episode in Marseilles where Carlo meets Pépé's mother, and significantly changes the overt nature of Pépé's criminal activities. Pépé's sordid activities in the novel, prostitution and drug trafficking, become, less contentiously, bank robbery and burglary, and the prostitute Inès becomes a housewife (although, as we will see later, Pépé's identity as pimp resurfaces in less explicit ways). Because of Gabin's genuine working-class image, Pépé's desire for Gaby's jewels in the film posits his criminal desires as the legitimate demands of an underclass wanting its share of wealth, shown to be in the hands of dour bourgeois colonialist Maxime, Gaby's sugar-daddy. Violence against women is equally displaced and cleaned up. While Ashelbé's Pépé beats Inès, in the film this role is left to Carlos, who is said to beat Tania. To fit Gabin's widely promoted Parisian origins, Pépé's are displaced from the lower depths of Marseilles, where his mother Ninette, an 'ugly, flat and sweaty' woman runs a sordid café, to the more salubrious working-class area of les Gobelins in Paris. Although Fréhel's Tania acts as a mother-substitute and therefore can be seen as a displacement of Ninette, the beauty and emotional power of her song lift her too above Ninette's sordid image.

Gabin's Pépé as a narrative creature thus owed as much to the star's persona in 1937 as to Ashelbé's thriller. As a visual representation, it takes to unprecedented heights the glamorisation of his face and general allure, achieved especially, as we have seen, by lighting. One of the best examples of this process takes place in his first meeting with Gaby in a young Arab woman's house, where Slimane has taken her to shelter during the police raid of the Casbah. The three of them are discussing the raid when a beat in the music and Gaby and Slimane's turned heads signal Pépé's arrival, shown first by a shot of his legs coming downstairs. When Pépé notices Gaby, their reciprocal fascination is translated into a classic pattern of shot/counter-shot. Pépé is as mesmerised by Gaby's jewels as by her face, and his point of view is expressed by lighting and framing: a close-up of her pearls is echoed by a close-up of her gleaming teeth. The remarkable aspect of this scene, however, is the degree to which Gabin's face is given the same treatment as Gaby's: as many close-ups and as much light.[24] His erotic status, already stated by Slimane ('when Pépé dies, there will be 3,000 widows at his funeral') is underlined by the lighting. Gabin's appeal to both men and women had been a feature of many of his previous films, where male homosocial bonding often took precedence over heterosexual romance, especially in Duvivier's *La Bandera* and *La Belle équipe*. In *Pépé le Moko*, this is given a particularly prominent treatment through the character of Slimane who plays a key intermediary role between Pépé and Gaby, and whose gaze obsessively follows Pépé. It is also a function of the film being a gangster movie, traditionally a male genre.

Pépé le Moko achieved a unique blend of French populist noir cinema and American gangster film, thereby laying the foundations for the French *policier* for decades to come. It is to this aspect of the film that we now turn.

2

. . . .

A FRENCH GANGSTER FILM

1. French vs American crime
Pépé le Moko was by no means the first French crime movie. There had been a steady silent production of mystery and adventure films, of which the most famous are Louis Feuillade's crime serials *Fantômas* (1913–14) and *Les Vampires* (1915–16). Duvivier himself had made several thrillers. *Pépé le Moko* is nevertheless a seminal film as the initiator of the French *gangster* film, setting the agenda for the *policier*[25] genre for decades to come. Many asked, upon its release, whether Duvivier had simply copied Hollywood. This was

historian Georges Sadoul's opinion: 'The film had no other ambition than to transpose American gangsters to another country. For the characterisation of the gang members, Duvivier was directly inspired by Howard Hawks and *Scarface*.'[26] It is true that the Hollywood gangster film made a big impact on the French public and critics, in particular Joseph von Sternberg's *Underworld* (1927), Howard Hawks's *Scarface*, Mervyn Le Roy's *Little Caesar* and William Wellman's *The Public Enemy* (all 1931), and that some key elements in *Pépé le Moko* are derived from its Hollywood predecessors: the gangster hero and his motley mob of hoodlums, the iconography of guns, sharp suits and felt hats, the glamorous 'moll'. As revealed by the French word *le gangster*, which appeared around 1925, this figure was perceived as quintessentially American. *Pépé le Moko*, however, reworks the Hollywood gangster figure and genre, producing a new hybrid which incorporates the specific literary, socio-cultural and cinematic features of French adaptations of crime literature and film noir.

Crime literature grew enormously in late 1920s and early 1930s France. Partly fuelled by the popularity of British and American writers, it also fostered new French-language authors – among them Georges Simenon and Léo Mallet – and new imprints such as Le Masque (from 1927). This expansion was accompanied, thanks to the development of photo-journalism, by a rise in sensationalist crime magazines, including the notorious Détective, founded in 1928. These publications gave crime increased visibility and glamour, while the country was shaken in the early 1930s by a series of high-profile scandals, especially those of bankers Albert Oustric and Marthe Hanau, and financial swindler Stavisky. Corsican gangs, modelled on the Mafia, began to dominate the French underworld, in Marseilles and Paris; the policemen say that Pépé 'tient le maquis' (has taken to the bush), a reference to Corsican bandits and thus indirectly to the Mafia. The French gangsters of the 1930s sported the new, Americanised, look of the sharp-suited, slicked-haired 'Latin' mobster typified by Paul Muni's Tony Camonte in Scarface. The new literary and cinematic developments, and the criminals themselves, thus spoke of American influence. At the same time, the French literary and cinematic expressions of the genre drew on indigenous traditions. One was the turn-of-the-century mystery and adventure novels – and silent film adaptations – of Gaston Leroux and Maurice Leblanc, with their bourgeois detectives and dapper gentlemen cambrioleurs (aristocratic burglars). Another was the degree to which the crime literature of the 1930s – of which Georges

Simenon is emblematic – showed more attention to 'atmosphere', to the depiction of a social milieu, than to solving crime. The first three Maigret films, Renoir's La Nuit du carrefour, Jean Tarride's Le Chien jaune, and Duvivier's La Tête d'un homme (all made in 1932) show how true this is also of the film adaptations. Pépé le Moko inherited this tradition. Pépé may rule over the Casbah like Chicago hoodlums over the Southside but, at the same time, as Graham Greene put it, Pépé le Moko is a film in which 'theme dominates incident'.[27] The Frenchness of Pépé le Moko in this respect resides in its skilful combination of French crime literature and film with the Hollywood gangster movie. The complexities of the film's negotiation of a new genre come into relief when it is compared with its illustrious Hollywood 'models', Scarface, Little Caesar and The Public Enemy.

Tony Camonte's motto in *Scarface*, 'Do it first, do it yourself and keep on doing it' and Rico's 'Shoot first' in *Little Caesar* contrast sharply with the lack of action in *Pépé le Moko*. Camonte, *Public Enemy*'s Tom Powers and *Little Caesar*'s Rico are always on the move, literally and metaphorically. They hit people in the face, ride in screeching cars, throw bombs, fire with machine-guns, wreck places. Powers robs a beer factory and viciously thrusts a grapefruit in his girlfriend's face. The filmic universe of the early Hollywood gangster movie acknowledges its link with the Western (Camonte strikes a match on the sheriff's star sported by one of the policemen) and the war film ('Gang War!' scream the newspaper headlines), two quintessential action genres. By contrast, *Pépé le Moko*, while predicated on the *identity* of the gangster, pays scant attention to his criminal *activities*.

The raid of the Casbah at the beginning of the film is (with the killing of Régis) the only conventional crime 'action' scene in the film. As such, it deserves attention. Several shots show the slow deployment of the police in the streets of the Casbah, the progress of informer Régis and the solidarity of the Casbah inhabitants who pretend to the police not to know Pépé; there is music but little dialogue. Régis tells Inès to 'warn' Pépé about the police, thus establishing Pépé's whereabouts, and passes the information on to the police. Inès warns Pépé, who understands he has been betrayed. There is a brief exchange of ineffectual gunshots between Pépé, his gang and the police from Grand Père's house, at the end of which Pépé is slightly wounded and takes refuge at a young Arab woman's house. The whole scene, which takes place at night, is under six minutes, of which only barely two are devoted

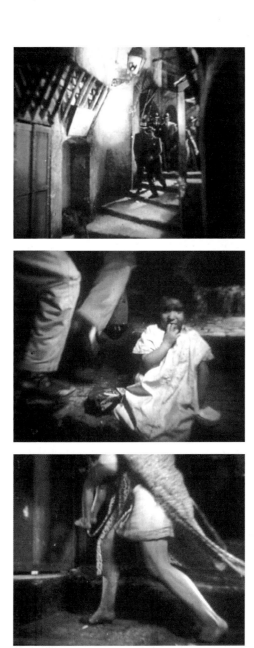

The police raid. Top: deployment in the Casbah streets; middle: the terrified child; bottom: the mother takes her child away to the rather perfunctory shooting. The progress of the police and Régis along the streets, accompanied by Scotto's elegiac, slow-pulsating orientalist music, is more evocative of a ballet than of a police raid. While the camera prowls furtively close to the walls, as if it were one of the inspectors, the policemen's deployment is prefaced by a series of knocks on doors which echo the beat of the music (they also connote the racist expression 'téléphone arabe', French for 'bush telephone'). Meanwhile, Pépé is stuck in Grand Père's house, positioned by an establishing high angle shot as trapped in a hole from where he will shoot a few desultory shots. The raid is more cat-and-mouse game than a confrontation between gangsters and the law. Pépé admits that he 'only aims at the legs' when shooting policemen, while they only succeed in wounding him superficially in the arm. No wonder the young Arab woman who shelters Slimane and Gaby, and later Pépé, shrugs and tells the startled Gaby that the whole thing is 'almost nothing'.

The scene also shows how its overt subject – the police raid – is a pretext for building up the 'atmosphere' of the Casbah introduced by the initial documentary-style montage. The music mixes Arabic song and Scotto's orientalist pastiche, with its low pitch, slow rhythm and lyrical violins. It creates a mood of sensuousness and nostalgia, of time suspended, which will develop throughout the whole film. With most camera angles on a slant (as in the montage), the Casbah appears as a mysterious and shady space, a dark labyrinth of tortuous streets and tumbling terraces. The third shot in the scene is exemplary of Duvivier's use of camera and décor. As policemen spread through the streets and people scurry inside doorways, a young child is left sitting on the street, crying, while policemen's legs rush past it, before its mother picks it up. The low-angle shot takes in details of crooked walls, dark doorways and, through lateral panoramic movement, two steeply inclined streets. The child provides a touch of the everyday, and the mother adds to the depiction of the Casbah as a sexualised space which began in the montage: the young woman's legs, contrasting with the policemen's, appear naked; she is wearing high-heel slippers, a short lacy slip and négligé, signalling her prostitute status.

In the American gangster films, there is usually a policeman intent on catching the hero: 'If it's the last thing I do' as Flaherty puts it in *Little Caesar*. In *Pépé le Moko* Slimane's goal is also to capture Pépé, but ever so slowly, '*chouia*, little by little, by attrition'. To the astonishment of his Parisian colleagues, he sees Pépé every day but does not arrest him. Rather, he 'wrote the date of his arrest on the sunny side of a wall'. Instead of the car chases of the Hollywood movies, Pépé and Slimane share leisurely strolls in the streets of the Casbah, pausing here to greet people, there to pick up food, as described in Chapter 1. While Slimane forever postpones Pépé's arrest, Pépé, himself a prisoner in the Casbah, is condemned to waiting for Pierrot, Gaby or Carlos to come to him, lounging in Inès' and Tania's flats, sitting in a room or in a café. Compared with Cagney's nervous energy in *The Public Enemy*, Paul Muni's resolve in *Scarface*, and to Edward G. Robinson's barely repressed violence in *Little Caesar*, Gabin is nonchalant. Pépé's angry outbursts at two fighters and a beggar after Pierrot's death are short in screen time and ritualised, expected as part of the Gabin performance style; his two descents to the harbour are almost balletic. While we see Camonte, Powers and Rico 'doing' crime, Pépé's criminal activities are in the past, evoked by the police or his acolytes, or in the future (they briefly plan a robbery), but never in the present, never on screen. This is particularly striking in view of the build-up Pépé is given by the policemen who state that he has killed five policemen, committed two bank raids and 33 burglaries, and been arrested 15 times. Duvivier's remark that 'the *policier* in the traditional sense does not interest me. In *La Tête d'un homme*, I expose all facts at the beginning […] I turned my film into a psychological study'[28] applies to *Pépé le Moko*. As in many later *policiers* of the 1940s and 1950s, crime is a pre-existing given rather than a topic to explore. To be a French criminal is existential rather than functional. It is also a pretext for imagery: Pépé's gun, which he casually takes out of his pocket when looking for his cigarettes, is a nod towards the genre's iconography. Neither fetishised machine nor lethal weapon, it functions almost as a fashion accessory.

The lack of action and the physical restraint which characterise *Pépé le Moko* correspond to a deeper sense of blockage. Compared to his American counterparts, this French gangster is an under-achiever. The American gangster's driving ambition, signalled by some of the titles (*Little Caesar*, *The Public Enemy*) is reiterated by dialogue: 'Some day I'm going to run the whole world. […] I'm going to write my name all over this town, and in big letters' (Camonte in *Scarface*); 'I'm taking over this territory' (Rico in *Little Caesar*). In the tradition of the classical, goal-oriented Hollywood heroes, the American gangsters start from the bottom of the ladder and make it to the top; *en route* they have to defeat and displace an older male figure, and the narrative is driven by this quest. By contrast, Pépé is already the boss, 'le *caïd* des *caïds*'. Men and women defer to him from the very beginning; he sorts out fights, eats and drinks where he chooses, and only needs to snap his fingers to get someone to escort Gaby out of the Casbah. He *is* the patriarchal figure, as his name 'Pépé' indicates. His trajectory can therefore only be downwards, graphically illustrated by the geography of the Casbah, from which he can only 'descend', a descent to death.

Pépé is trapped in the Casbah, as Inès triumphantly tells him: 'They want to arrest you, they don't realise it's already done!' It is not so much that Pépé has no goal or that his quest is without object, but that his goal is a regressive one; it consists of going back to the past. As Tania does through her song, Pépé wishes to return to Paris, to his childhood. In this, Pépé foreshadows the fate of many Poetic Realist protagonists (often embodied by Gabin), trapped heroes who dream of escaping to a mythical *ailleurs* (elsewhere). Jacques in *La Bête humaine* wants to escape the legacy of his alcoholic forebears; Pepel in *Les Bas-fonds* wants a vague 'something else'; François in *Le Jour se lève* fantasises about the Côte d'azur, Jean in *Le Quai des brumes* about Latin America (in the latter film he too gets on a boat at the end, but leaves it and is killed). These dreams all fail; as Séverine tells Jacques in *La Bête humaine*, 'ahead of [you], it's blocked'. *Pépé le Moko* expresses this sense of blockage more acutely than these other films because Pépé is already 'elsewhere'. In this respect he resembles the hero of Jacques Feyder's 1934 *Le Grand jeu* (played by Pierre Richard-Wilm), who joins the Foreign Legion in Morocco to escape his past, but is relentlessly drawn back to it by a woman who is a disturbing double of the woman he left behind. In *Pépé le Moko* women play a similar symbolic role, emphasising the Oedipal nature of the hero's blockage. Gaby is the lure of Paris as glamorous object of desire, Tania its flipside, the nostalgia for the maternal 'lost' city. Editing and camerawork reinforce the blocking symbolism of the women: in contrast to the mobility of the camera in the rest of the film, Pépé's first meeting with Gaby is marked by an alternation of lingering, static shots/counter-shots, while Tania's song is covered in two very long, static shots.

Pépé le Moko's narrative structure reinforces its sense of doom and entrapment. Each of Pépé's significant actions is foreshadowed by himself or

Doomed dreams of escape. Top: Pépé on the terrace with Inès (Line Noro);
middle: Inès stops Pépé's descent to the harbour; bottom: Pépé trapped in Tania's room

one of his acolytes. There are two significant letters (the fake letter to Pierrot, Pépé's letter to Gaby – both of which lead to death), two ritual punishments by Pépé (of Régis and of L'Arbi), two song scenes (Pépé's and Tania's), two montages (at the beginning and over Pépé's song), and two displays of Pépé's depression, after Pierrot's death and after Gaby's failure to return a second time. Pépé's final escape is anticipated several times. There is Pépé's own first attempt at leaving the Casbah midway through the film, and there are Pierrot's, and later Carlos's departures and subsequent arrest or death. Police informers Régis and L'Arbi both return to meet their punishment after their excursions outside the Casbah; Pépé kills Régis and beats L'Arbi. This network of rhymes and repetitions builds up a strong sense of fate and inevitability and provides poetic motivation, where realistic motivation is weak (for instance, why should Pierrot, a petty bank thief, be shot by the police?). Through these mirrored and repeated actions, the film constructs a strong sense of poetic entrapment and of the deathly power of the Casbah.

Throughout the 1930s, Gabin's filmography is dominated by melodramatic victims, doomed heroes who do not control their fate. Although in the same period others incarnated such heroes (for instance, Jean-Louis Barrault, Pierre Blanchar, Pierre Richard-Wilm), Gabin became the emblem of a pervasive sense of doom and pessimistic vision of society. If the Hollywood gangster seems almost parodically to express the drive of the self-made American hero, Gabin's Pépé appears as the perfect expression of a blocked French society turned towards its past. Having said this, we should be cautious about too direct a connection between film and society, for at the same time comedies and musicals were just as popular as the more serious genres. For instance, in 1937, *Pépé le Moko* was outperformed at the box-office by Fernandel's comic operetta *Ignace*. Like Duvivier and Gabin's previous film *La Belle équipe*, *Pépé le Moko* was made at the time of the Popular Front and this political context is relevant to an understanding of the film, especially in relation to the colonial setting (as will be discussed in Chapter 3). But Pépé's identity is highly mediated as we have seen: by Gabin's star image, by Hollywood gangster movies, by earlier French crime novels and films. Pépé also has a more overt, politically motivated ancestor, that of the Parisian *apache*.

The nineteenth-century *roman populaire*, epitomised by Eugène Sue's 1842 *Les Mystères de Paris* established a vision of crime in the city which lived on through Emile Zola's naturalist novel and the populist

literature of the 1920s and 1930s. This literature forged an amalgalm
between the working classes and the underworld, which has endured.
The conflation of 'dangerous' and 'labouring' classes derived from the
bourgeoisie's fear of the new urban workforce, especially in Paris, seen
as ridden with crime, violence and disease. As historian Louis Chevalier
put it, 'the proletariat and its living conditions [were] described as
analogous to wild savages,'[29] hence the term *apache*. The trope of the
apache, then, fundamentally criminalises the working class, shifting
social oppression on to individual crime. The habitat of the *apache* and
of his various linguistic incarnations – *voyou*, *escarpe*, *mauvais garçon*
(Gaby's friend Gravère at one point calls Pépé 'cette grande escarpe') –
is the melting pot of working and criminal classes, the *zone* and the
popular *quartiers*, archetypally Montmartre and Pigalle. In the 1920s and
1930s, film-makers such as Duvivier, Renoir, Carné and Chenal,
together with writers, singers and photographers, perpetuated the
working-class / low-life amalgam. Simenon's novels used crime fiction
to observe popular milieux, while most populist writers, notably Pierre
MacOrlan and Francis Carco (who both supplied texts for French 1930s
cinema as well as crime magazines) were chiefly interested in the
proletariat's criminal fringes. The eponymous hero of Fritz Lang's
French film *Liliom* (1934) is such a *mauvais garçon*, embodied by Charles
Boyer, who some critics saw as a precursor for Pépé, though the only
direct similarity is that he kills himself with a knife (later on,
commentators may have been influenced by the fact that Boyer plays
Pépé in the 1938 remake *Algiers*). Closer to Pépé in this respect are other
Gabin films, especially *Paris-Béguin*, *Coeur de Lilas*, and *Les Bas-fonds*.
Pépé's *apache* ancestry is evoked in his mythical meeting place with
Gaby, the place Blanche, an area of Paris described by the Michelin guide
as 'straight out of Carco's novels'. The mythology of the *apache* was
pervasive. The 18 March 1937 issue of the fan magazine *Pour Vous*
dubbed the Pépé–Gaby romance 'l'amour *apache*', and *Ciné-Miroir* of 19
February 1937 ran a page on Gabin as a typical '*mauvais garçon*'. Outside
France, the *apache* became one of the stereotypical representations of
the French working-class thug. In the late 1920s and early 1930s a
Hollywood agency commissioned two Parisian photographers, the
Séeberger brothers, to take photographs of typical Parisian locations as
models for film décors. While most were of luxury hotels, night spots
and restaurants, others were of ordinary cafés and '*apache* houses'.[30] The

le mauvais garçon

alla chanter à Rio-de-Janeiro. Pour un paresseux, ce fut une jeunesse bien remplie. Il eut de grands succès au théâtre. Cependant il le délaissa pour le cinéma. La première proposition qui lui fut faite vint de Berlin, mais c'est à Paris qu'il débuta. On le vit dans un grand nombre de films qu'il serait fastidieux d'énumérer ; il remporta surtout de grands succès dans *la Belle Marinière, Maria Chapdelaine* et *la Bandera*. Il aime à parler de cette dernière œuvre.

Pensez donc qu'il m'a fallu aller présenter le film à Rouen, confiait-il, dans son langage imagé, à un reporter. C'était la première fois que j'essayais ce boulot, et j'avais un peu le trac, car, si j'ai l'habitude du public comme acteur, je ne suis pas précisément orateur, et j'avais la gorge un peu serrée ; enfin, ça s'est très bien arrangé. Pierre Mac Orlan est venu à mon secours très gentiment ; c'est lui qui a fait tout le discours ; moi, je me suis contenté de dire aux Rouennais ce qui me passait par la tête... Je leur ai parlé de leur équipe de football dont ils sont si fiers à juste titre. Je leur ai dit que je venais pour la première fois dans leur ville que je trouvais sympathique, et eux aussi. Et puis, c'est tout. Ils sont vraiment chic, ils ne m'ont pas emboîté !

Mais Jean Gabin n'aime pas beaucoup parler de son travail. Il aime bien le studio, mais il préfère les sports et, en particulier, ceux qui se pratiquent dans l'air vif des montagnes. Tous les ans, il retourne à Megève. Mais il descend dans un petit hôtel tranquille, parce qu'il a horreur des palaces. Sa distraction préférée, c'est la chasse. A Paris, il se délasse en allant faire chaque matin un petit tour au Bois. Tout le long des Acacias, des quantités de gens qu'il ne connaît pas du tout, le saluent comme une vieille connaissance, et il leur répond avec sérieux ; c'est une distraction comme une autre. Il ne tarit pas d'éloges lorsqu'il parle des Américains ; il les a vus à l'œuvre, et il en a gardé un excellent souvenir. Il a été frappé par la collaboration complète et parfaite entre les acteurs et les producteurs dans les studios d'Hollywood.

— Là-bas, dit-il, les auteurs du dialogue facilitent la tâche de leurs interprètes en leur prêtant le langage qui leur convient. Ici, ce n'est pas toujours la même chose. Les auteurs de dialogues en France ont, malgré eux, le culte du beau langage, de la phrase bien balancée.

Heureusement, que Jean Gabin est là pour bousculer les textes et les adapter à son personnage.

— Un contremaître d'usine, a-t-il l'habitude d'expliquer, un gars des faubourgs ne doivent cependant pas s'expliquer comme un académicien ou un avocat : chaque métier a son argot pittoresque, expressif. Pour faire vrai, l'essentiel est de parler exactement comme les gens qu'on doit représenter, sinon c'est du chiqué, et le public ne s'y trompe pas. Il ne faut pas croire que, pour faire nature, il suffise de parler argot.

C'est très difficile à manier l'argot, quand on en a pas l'habitude.

Heureusement pour nous, Jean Gabin en a l'habitude.

RÉMY GARRIGUES.

Mireille Ballin et Jean Gabin,
dans « Pépé le Moko ».

Une expression de Jean Gabin,
dans « Les Bas-Fonds ».

Jean GABIN

Brigitte Helm et Jean Gabin, dans « Adieu, les beaux jours ».

JEAN GABIN est parmi les vedettes d'aujourd'hui l'une des plus aimées du public. C'est le garçon costaud que les femmes aimeraient avoir pour confident et consolateur, les hommes pour ami sûr et durable. Comme on l'a dit, il a créé à l'écran un personnage bien à lui : le mauvais garçon au bon cœur. C'est un gars de Paname, qui a été élevé à la dure, et qui a gardé le vocabulaire de sa jeunesse. Il est d'une pièce, cordial, simple, sain, un philosophe à sa manière. En ce moment, il est mêlé, dans *Bas-Fonds* et dans *Pépé le Moko*, à de sombres aventures. C'est qu'il en a eu dans la vie. Ne pouvant pas supporter la discipline du lycée, il s'en évada, et le voilà parti sur la grand'route à la recherche d'une situation et d'un morceau de pain. C'est ainsi qu'il devint aide-forgeron. Taper sur l'enclume, c'était du sport ; ensuite, il fit son service militaire dans la marine. A son retour, l'enfant prodigue s'assagit, et, cédant aux instances de son frère, il fit un tour de chant aux Folies-Bergère, puis au Moulin-Rouge, ensuite aux Bouffes-Parisiens. Entre temps, il

The fan magazine *Ciné-Miroir* of 19 February 1937 features Gabin as 'le mauvais garçon'

Italian spoof *Totó le Mokó* has its star Totó perform a '*danse apache*' (see Chapter 4).

The *apache* is a contradictory figure, at the same time belonging to his class and yet marginal to it, a contradiction fundamental to Pépé's and Gabin's identity. We are told that Pépé was a 'cabinet maker'. This choice endows him with the virtues of the artisan, who loves a job well done, respects property and cares for the objects he steals, as opposed to Carlos who butchers them. This makes Pépé an attractive figure, a criminal who is not anti-social. Whereas early nineteenth-century representations of the urban labourer put the accent on his ugliness, later visions romanticised and embellished him. They also eroticised him. Brassaï's photographs of *The Secret Paris of the '30s*, Carco's *Jésus la Caille* and films such as *Paris-Béguin* and *Coeur de Lilas* all exploit the erotic appeal of the hoodlum. Ashelbé's *Pépé le Moko* is no exception. When describing his first encounter with Pépé, his friend Carlo, while noting the sordid surrounding, remarks that 'he was really seductive'. Lighting, camerawork and clothes likewise enhance Pépé's seductiveness and strong erotic appeal. When her girlfriend asks for a description of Pépé, Gaby replies: 'sympathetic ... and frightening'. The expression on her face at that point, shot in close-up, and the glowing light which envelops her (as well as her girlfriend in the preceding shot) leave the spectator in no doubt as to Pépé's erotic appeal.

2. Masculine display

The paradox of the gangster film is that it allows for a highly narcissistic display of the male body, while preserving a virile image of 'rugged masculinity'. Successful gangsters must have sharp outfits. Camonte in *Scarface* proudly acquires a silk dressing-gown similar to that of his boss and shows off his numerous shirts to Poppy (the boss's girl-friend). We see Tom Powers being fitted for his first suit in *The Public Enemy* and in the same film 'Nails' Nathan is the image of the dandy. In *Little Caesar*, Rico closely examines his hero Pete Montana's outfit, including his jewels; his spats are prominently displayed as he puts his feet on a desk. *Pépé le Moko* adopts similar codes of masculine display, combining the iconography of French working-class masculinity, Hollywood gangsters and contemporary fashion trends. It uses the North African décor and clothing as a foil to the Western modernity of its heroes.

Ashelbé introduces Pépé in the book as someone who is 'careful about his appearance: a collar-less shirt as is *de rigueur*, but a suit worn with ease, and, above all, impeccable white shoes'. Duvivier and Gabin slightly changed Pépé's clothes but kept him 'natty', as Graham Greene put it. The first time we see him, Pépé is wearing a glowing – probably silk – light-coloured tie with dark polka dots, over a dark shirt. The motif of the dots returns at the end of the film, in the scarf he wears for his descent to the harbour. Pépé's scarf has tiny dark circles on light fabric, the reverse of the dark scarf with white spots worn by Gaby as she stands on the ship's deck, pursuing the theme of a mirror relationship between the two characters (she also wears her hat in a similar way to his). This detail shows the care taken in the choice of clothes for Pépé and the attention paid to 'hoodlum fashion'. Pépé's clothes are smart. Their neatness and straight lines contrast with the crumpled outfits of Régis and of the Arab characters (Slimane, L'Arbi), with the nondescript suits of the policemen and with Grand Père's floppy patterned sweater and top coat. When others are fanning themselves and sweat inelegantly, Pépé is crisp in light-coloured suit and shirt and white cuffs, for example when he comes out of Inès' house after their row. His hair is always slicked back, allowing light to reflect on it; the only exception is in the scene after Pierrot's funeral, when he is, briefly, dishevelled. When planning the robbery, Pépé's attire of light-coloured shirt, grey jacket and dark tie is close to a business suit. In this, he and Duvivier followed new trends in men's fashion which saw the arrival, partly via Hollywood, of the 'London cut' smart suits, the jacket with wide shoulders and wide lapels, and baggy trousers usually with turn-ups. This style was quickly adopted by movie stars, businessmen and bandits. As poet Blaise Cendrars put it: 'The bandit seen on the Champs-Elysées in 1935 is above all a businessman, just like his Chicago counterpart.'[31] Underworld fashion, however, distorted and exaggerated the new outfits because, as fashion historian Farid Chenoune explains, hoodlum chic 'far from operating as camouflage, ultimately functioned like warrior dress'.[32] Pépé's clothes are a cunning blend of the smart businessman and the villain. The well-cut jackets with discreetly patterned fabric, baggy trousers and dark tie over light-coloured shirt, declare in their sobriety the 'straight' aspect of his activities (Pierrot, Pépé's spiritual heir, is also dressed in a sober dark suit). It is left to Jimmy (Modot) to embody the vulgar mobster with his caricaturally

Masculine display: Pépé dresses up to go to his tragic
death in the harbour

garish checked jacket and bow-tie and to Carlos to represent 'working-classness' with a looser, casual top under his jacket and the archetypal cloth cap, contrasting with Pépé's smart hat. On the other hand, Pépé's *soignée* elegance, his two-tone shoes, soft felt hat worn on a slant, light-coloured tie over black shirt and the rather raffish spotted scarf, discreetly connote the pimp, even though the film in other ways suppresses this aspect of the book's character. The figure was familiar from films, photographs and novels such as Carco's *Jésus la Caille*, and the audience, it seems, got the message. André Brunelin, Gabin's biographer, claims that 'after *Pépé le Moko*, Jean was assailed with offers from prostitutes who wished to "work" with him'.[33] However authentic the anecdote, fashion clearly played an important role in fleshing out the character of Pépé.

Gabin was known for the care he took in choosing clothes, both for his roles and in real life. Michèle Morgan, his co-star in *Le Quai des brumes*, was surprised, on first meeting him, by his 'bourgeois elegance'[34] compared to his working-class screen image. Earlier films, notably *Paris-Béguin* and *Coeur de Lilas*, had given Gabin the opportunity to display the characteristic smartness of the crook/pimp. In *Coeur de Lilas* he plays a small but arresting role, that of a *mauvais garçon* in the *louche* Parisian café in which a bourgeois policeman (André Luguet) is conducting an undercover investigation. Gabin cuts a sinister but dashing figure, in felt hat – while other men, again, wear cloth caps – and a striking white scarf crossed over his chest like the spotted scarf at the end of *Pépé le Moko*. This beautiful (and underrated) film is also premonitory in teaming Gabin with Fréhel, as they both sing, in turn, a rather bawdy song, 'La môme caoutchouc'. With *Pépé le Moko*, Gabin could give full scope to his sartorial elegance. When he sits back at Chani's café, depressed at Pierrot's death, his jacket opens to reveal a discreet 'JG' monogram on his black shirt. The fact that he wore his own shirt may not have been spotted by all spectators (it is more or less invisible on video) and it may have nothing to do with the practice of French crooks who, as Chenoune tells us, 'had their own suppliers … Séverin, the Marseilles shirtmaker specialized in silk shirts with the mobsters' initials embroidered on the breast'.[35] Nevertheless, clothes in *Pépé le Moko*, as signalled by the monogrammed shirt, allow for a particularly felicitous merging of the star with the character. Brunelin states that Pépé's spotted scarf and the way it is worn, 'gave this

The French gangster's 'family of men': (from left to right) Pierrot (Gilbert-Gil), Pépé, Max (Roger Legris), Jimmy (Gaston Modot), Carlos (Gabriel Gabrio) and Grand Père (Saturnin Fabre)

The romantic gangster: a publicity still of Jean Gabin and Mireille Balin as Pépé and Gaby   45

accessory such an aura that in the months that followed the release of *Pépé le Moko*, many men, including of course Pigalle's pimps, wore it in a similar way'.[36]

Since the identity of the pimp, with its implications of sleaze and dependency on women, was too derogatory for the Gabin image, why did the film nevertheless keep a sartorial style that connoted that figure? One answer lies in the prevalence of the pimp in the populist culture on which *Pépé le Moko* drew. In the novel of *Pépé le Moko*, Inès is prostitute to Pépé's pimp, and in many of Fréhel's songs, the pimp–prostitute pair is the archetypal couple, often characterised by violence (a trace of which survives in Tania telling Pépé, 'I've always been beaten'). Another answer is the aura of sexuality which this identity brings to the characters. Gaby, the kept woman, is a 'higher' form of prostitute, of which she bluntly reminds her protector during their row. As we will see in Chapter 4, the remake *Algiers* removes this aspect from the relationship and makes Gaby and Maxime 'fiancés'. Equally, the 'shadow' of the pimp on Pépé emphasises the sexual aura of the *apache*. This may be why Pépé's elegant shoes, emblematic of the pimp, are intensely fetishised from his spectacular entrance into the young Arab woman's house (filmed in close-ups of his feet descending stairs), to the shot of him sitting on the edge of the terrace after his first meeting with Gaby, which displays his shoes like a fashion shot, and the shots of his feet on his last descent to the harbour at end of the film.

3. Pépé's male family

The adaptation of Ashelbé's novel almost entirely invented Pépé's gang. Where the book focuses on Pépé and Carlo(s), Duvivier and his scriptwriters fleshed out the gang, introduced the young Pierrot and the two informers Régis and L'Arbi, thereby creating several sub-plots, but also providing Duvivier's favoured milieu of 'men's stories'.

Pépé lords over a motley group of acolytes: young Pierrot, brutish Carlos, idiotically smiling Max and man-with-the-*bilboquet* Jimmy; on the periphery of the group is Grand Père. The group, as Sadoul claimed, is reminiscent of *Scarface*; Jimmy's play with his *bilboquet* a direct transposition of George Raft throwing his coin. The French group, however, is more explicitly modelled on a traditional family.[37] The first scene which follows the Casbah montage establishes the cohesion of the group as well as Pépé's status as *caïd*. As the men discuss the spoils of their latest burglary, a ritualistic exchange of ironic phrases between Pépé and Carlos ('tu m' fais mal' – 'you're hurting me') and the other men's approval of Pépé's opinion, cement the group and establish his undisputed command. Composition and framing reinforce his central, dominant position. This heralds the manner in which the men will 'shadow' Pépé throughout the film, exaggerating, anticipating or repeating his actions, either verbally or visually: most shots of Pépé in the cafés and streets of the Casbah feature one or two members of the group in the background or on the edges, especially Max and Jimmy. The cohesion of the group is visually reiterated in the two card games and culminates in the killing of Régis, to which Pépé has summoned everyone. While he and Carlos hold the dying Pierrot up, Carlos shoots from the gun held in Pierrot's hand. Relationships among the men are explicitly familial: Grand Père, the oldest member, proffers wise advice in the manner worthy of his name, and treats Carlos like an impatient child. Pépé plays father to the group, and, symbolically, father and mother to Pierrot. His stern words or slap in the face to Pierrot are always accompanied by a show of affection. The accent on a strong father–son relationship at the centre of the group will be a constant feature of *policiers* such as *Touchez pas au Grisbi* (1954), *Bob le flambeur* (1956), and *Mélodie en sous-sol* (1969), while it is absent from *Pépé le Moko*'s remakes. The familial nature of the group of men also arises from its relationship with its habitat. The men's familiarity with the streets and cafés of the Casbah derives first of all from the fact that, unhampered by actual criminal activities, they spend more time there than their American counterparts. Secondly, the restricted space of the Casbah, contrasting with the wider urban spaces of the US gangster films, reinforces the sense of a known topography, similar in this to a Parisian *quartier* such as Montmartre or Pigalle. But the nature of the relationship is different too. Rather than violently taking over alien territory or tearing through anonymous urban space as in so many American films noirs, Pépé and his men are completely at home in the Casbah, where inhabitants protect them from the police, and sing along with Pépé's songs. This is one reason why the film starts with a map and portrait of the Casbah, in the same way as *Bob le flambeur* starts with a description of Montmartre and Pigalle. In this film as well as post-war *policiers*, the familiarity of the men with their *quartier* is always carefully established by the use of real names for streets, squares and cafés, and woven into the plot. As we saw earlier on in the account of Pépé and Slimane's walk through the Casbah, the film establishes a physical closeness between the men and their habitat, echoing their mental relationship to it. This brings the French gangsters into the realm of the quotidian, countering their extraordinary status and visual identity.

While the group aims to reproduce a family, it does so, however, without women. Pépé dispenses 'motherly' advice and affection to Pierrot, but women do not partake of this affection. In fact, Pierrot models his behaviour on Pépé's in his relationship to women too. Pépé telling Inès sharply to 'go back home!' after she has warned him, albeit unwittingly, of Régis' betrayal, is echoed by Pierrot barking 'home!' to Aïcha after she has brought him a letter. Mère Tarte's only narrative function is to provide a room for receiving Gaby (we might compare the food connotations of 'tarte' with those of 'Madame Bouche' who plays a not dissimilar function in *Touchez pas au grisbi*). Inès is seen cooking, but her couscous will not be eaten by Pépé who, instead, looks for home and solace in cafés. The treatment of women in *Pépé le Moko* is in line with Duvivier's other misogynist all-male group films – such as *La Bandera* and *La Belle équipe* – but this feature endures beyond the director's work. Pépé's later incarnations in the heroes of *Bob le flambeur* and *Touchez pas au grisbi* and other post-war *policiers* also head male families that exclude women and look for surrogate homes in bars and cafés.

Pépé le Moko establishes for the posterity of the French genre the paradox of a male group whose relationships are less brutal, more tender and homely and thus more 'feminine' than in the Hollywood gangster films, but from which women are still excluded. In particular the hero's mother, who plays a central role in *Scarface* and *The Public Enemy*, is here absent – even though Pépé's mother figures in the novel. Women in *Pépé le Moko* are erotic object (Gaby), marginal nurturing figures (Inès, Tania, Mère Tarte) or go-betweens (Inès, Pierrot's girlfriend). Their presence remains structurally peripheral to the homosocial bonds between the men. The blurred border between homosocial and homoerotic is illustrated by the way the Pépé–Slimane couple mirrors that of Pépé and Gaby. Pépé's desire for Gaby is matched by Slimane's desire to catch Pépé, but also by Slimane's obsession with the erotic exchanges between Pépé and Gaby. Slimane watches Pépé and Gaby enter the house where they will make love with a wistful expression, paces up and down the street while they are in the house, and appreciatively looks at his watch when they come out, in the same way as he had overheard Inès' declaration of love to Pépé. Though his job is to keep watch over Pépé, his repeated motto that he wants to capture Pépé 'slowly, slowly', which provokes the wrath of his superiors, suggests the ritualistic pleasure of courtship in postponing the moment of conquest, rather than the call of professional duty. The ambivalent nature of the relationship between the two men, though disavowed through their repeated vows of mutual hostility, is expressed by their physical closeness in the frame and the language they use ('my little chicken … my little pheasant'). Slimane's betrayal of Gaby and Pépé's relationship to Maxime, while part of his policeman's plan, can also be seen as an act of jealousy at his exclusion from the couple. However, while the film thus suggests the possibility of desire by one man for another, this desire is mocked and denied in the treatment of Slimane by Pépé, while the heterosexual erotic relationship triumphs in the Pépé–Gaby couple.

4. A romantic gangster

Love, spurned or marginalised as 'soft stuff' (Rico in *Little Caesar*) in the Hollywood gangster film, is triumphant in *Pépé le Moko*. The film keeps the book's basic narrative line: Slimane introducing Gaby to Pépé, using her to lure him out of the Casbah, Pépé's final arrest and suicide. The adaptation, however, extended Pépé and Gaby's one brief exchange and sordid sexual encounter in a back yard into three romantic rendezvous. But despite the extended romance, tight plotting has led many viewers and critics to perceive the film's temporal span as two days, rather than the five days over which the story actually unfolds. Days 1, 2 and 3 of story time are each marked by Pépé and Gaby coming together: at the young Arab woman's house on Day 1, at café Ali Baba on Day 2 and at Mère Tarte's on Day 3. Pépé and Gaby's dance on Day 2, a visual displacement of their lovemaking, takes place exactly halfway through the film. Days 4 and 5, which occupy less screen time, centre on their frustrated attempts to meet, as the law (Slimane and Maxime) keeps them apart. On Day 4, Pépé waits in vain for Gaby as she is trapped at Hotel Aletti, thinking him dead. On Day 5, they are reunited spatially at the harbour, but more than ever divided: first by the window of the ship's bar, then by the ship itself. Pépé, handcuffed behind the rails of the harbour, watches the ship take Gaby away, as its deafening horn drowns his voice calling out her name. Gaby puts her hands over her ears, wincing at the noise, symbolically blocking Pépé's call. This imaginative use of sound sums up the conflation of desire and loss, a theme which has been running through the film and is clearly expressed through the Pépé–Gaby–Pierrot triangle. As Pépé's desire for Gaby grows, so he loses Pierrot. The climactic moment of the dance is literally embedded in the long sequence of Régis' punishment for his betrayal (and indirectly killing) of Pierrot. Pépé and his acolytes gather in the backroom at café Ali Baba (also called L'Algérien) to make Régis talk about Pierrot's whereabouts, when Pépé is called out because of the arrival of Gaby and her friends. In turn, the arrival of the dying Pierrot at the bar takes Pépé away from Gaby. After Régis has been killed in retribution for Pierrot's death, Pépé finds the bar empty. Pépé's depression following Pierrot's death in Day 3 finds an echo in his depression at Gaby's failure to return on Day 4. Pépé's pursuit of Gaby triggers off his own death. This tragic vision of love marks the film as belonging to the 'intemporal' romantic tradition, where love and death are intimately linked and where the lovers' ultimate separation is a sign of the greatness of their passion. But Pépé and Gaby's love is also very much of the 1930s.

Gaby's glamorous looks are a vision of the luxury Paris with which she identifies (the Champs-Elysées) as well as Hollywood cinema for a French audience. Mireille Balin, a former model, is the epitome of the elegant *Parisienne* whose plucked eyebrows denote the beauty salon, and who wears a different, carefully chosen couture outfit for each occasion: long white evening dress with white fur on the first night; white satin top and long black skirt on the second night; grey and flowery 'afternoon' suits with shorter skirts; white coat, white hat and black spotted scarf on the ship. While obeying the canons of 1930s women's fashion (the varying skirts' lengths for each moment of the day correctly follow 1930s women's fashion codes), the clothes also speak of impractical luxury and mark her out as alien to her surroundings. Gaby's visual beauty, however, like Pépé's, covers her more sordid existence and humble origins, and she attracts Pépé precisely because of this duality, as a projection of his own desires and split identity. Her association with jewels begins with the camera's exchange of close-ups of her face, neck and arms, with those of Pépé's gaze at them. When she tells him that before having jewels she desired them, she confirms her status as his double. They both desire wealth and are prepared to do anything for it. Typical of gender stereotyping, her means are sexual, his are criminal. As the film develops, Pépé loses interest in her jewels, much to Carlos's chagrin. Sexual desire has taken over, but more importantly her function as nostalgic reminder of working-class Paris has displaced the luxury image. One of Pépé's last lines to her is: 'You're covered in silk, full of gold, and you remind me of the Métro, *frites* and cups of *café-crème* on café terraces.'

The woman's function as object of male desire and projection of his fantasies is classic in mainstream cinema. What is special to *Pépé le Moko* (and many other Gabin films) is the degree to which the woman is coded, quite explicitly, as his double rather than his opposite. So while *Pépé le Moko* prefigures 1940s and 1950s American film noir in its criminal milieu, atmosphere and lighting, Gaby is no *femme fatale*. As the ending's 'reverse' scarves shows, she is too familiar (the Métro), too close (they both come from les Gobelins). She is the pretext and justification for Pépé's tragic journey, not its fundamental reason. Pépé knows that his regressive trajectory can only lead to death. His dressing up for it in his scarf and hat is the last knowing gesture of a doomed romantic. Like Cyrano de Bergerac, he is ultimately a loser; but there is no gainsaying his panache.

. . . .

Such noir glamour and romanticism attached to a hoodlum was bound to attract criticism, though this criticism was ambivalent, as it also recognised the artistic and technical mastery and the emotional power of the film. Unusually in the French context, the criticism of the noir element of *Pépé le Moko* did not follow neat political lines. Echoing some of the contemporary reviews of the film, right-wing historians Maurice Bardèche and Robert Brasillach, who otherwise liked the film, regretted '[t]he rather low fashion for hoodlums and cowards which [*Pépé le Moko*'s] success provoked'.[38] But the left-wing weekly *Marianne* also wrote, at the release of Pierre Chenal's 1939 *Le Dernier tournant* (the first film version of *The Postman Always Rings Twice*), 'Here is another film noir, one of this sinister series which starts with *Les Bas-fonds* and *Crime et châtiment* and continues with *Pépé le Moko* and *Quai des brumes*, *La Bête humaine* and *Hôtel du Nord*.'[39]

Apart from noting that many of the critics who attacked French film noir before the war became those who sang the praises of American film noir afterwards, we cannot engage here in the complex debates that the genre generated in France. We may remark, however, on the fact that such criticism addressed ideology (especially in relation to the impeding war) rather than morals. And indeed, in the film itself, traditional morality is flouted to the indifference of the French censors. Like *Scarface*, *The Public Enemy* and *Little Caesar*, *Pépé le Moko* glorifies the hoodlum, but unlike them makes no apology for it. No words of moral warning precede it (such as those of *Scarface* and *The Public Enemy*) and the films' endings are exemplary in this respect. Tony Camonte suffers a drawn-out agony; he is shot in his flat under a hail of bullets, staggers downstairs, falls in the gutter. Tom Powers is wrapped in bandages on a hospital bed, then kidnapped and brought back to his mother as a ghastly mummy. Rico falls into the gutter, mowed down by police machine-guns. By contrast, Pépé directs the *mise-en-scène* of his own death. He chooses the place and means, whereas in both *Algiers* and *Casbah* he is shot by the police (Vichy censorship manipulated the ending of *Pépé le Moko* in 1942, to make it appear as punishment but the original ending was restored at the Liberation).[40] The hero of *Pépé le Moko* dies for poetic reasons, not because crime must be punished.

But why does this have to take place in Algiers? Contemporary reviews and later historians' commentaries linked *Pépé le Moko* to such other noir classics as *La Bête humaine*, *Le Quai des brumes* and *Le Jour se lève*, all set in contemporary urban France. Is the Casbah setting a simple exotic backdrop to pursue the same themes as the other films, or does it fundamentally affect the meaning of the story?

3

. . . .

A TALE OF TWO CITIES: ALGIERS AND PARIS

Algeria! ... For Carlo the word designated a confusion of things. He remembered images, spectacles and tales and he readily pictured a lewd Orient, full of traffickers and odalisques. He felt towards the country a kind of superior contempt. [...] For, if he ignores Algiers, he knows the Casbah. He is informed about the old barbaresque citadel, now an extraordinary labyrinth ruled by outlaws. (Ashelbé, *Pépé le Moko*)[41]

1. Colonial culture

This quote from Ashelbé's book sums up the mixture of prejudice and fantasy evoked by North Africa in the French popular imaginary, manifested by the 1931 *Exposition coloniale* where 'visitors could barter in Tunisian and Algerian souks' and 'under the guise of folkloric presentations, veiled Algerian women danced before a titillated French public'.[42] Since conquest in 1830, France had commercial, military and political interests in Algeria, as well as cultural ambitions: the so-called *mission civilisatrice*. By the 1930s, French culture was redolent with colonialism, channelled into a variety of discourses, from facile or sophisticated exoticism to plain racism.

This culture had a 'noble' ancestry: the tradition of orientalist painting (notably Delacroix), Musset and Baudelaire's poetry, novels from Flaubert's Salambô to Gide's L'Immoraliste. Then there was also a more popular streak, with writers such as Pierre Loti, and populist novelists frequently used the colonies as setting; Pierre MacOrlan and Georges Simenon to name but two. In typical orientalist fashion, most of these texts presented a dual vision of the colonial space: dangerous and repellent, but alluring and desirable. The new mass media followed suit. Exhibitions, popular songs, tourist brochures, advertising and postcards appropriated the beauties of colonial landscape and people. To wit the following advertisement for the Algerian Railways, describing the country as 'the first film studio in the world', praising 'the magnificent panoramas that can be admired during a trip to Algeria, which will be represented at the Algerian Railway Stand in the Pavillon du Tourisme Nord-Africain at the Colonial Exhibition, in the form of revolving luminous tableaux and dioramas'.[43] Tourism and commerce form a discreet sub-text to *Pépé le Moko*. The reason that Gaby and her friends can consume the exoticism of the Casbah is because Maxime is on a business trip to sell his champagne; the maître d'hôtel of the Hotel Aletti introduces him to Slimane as 'Monsieur Kleep. Kleep, des champagnes'. Though this point is more developed in the book than in the film, the precise designation of Maxime's activities connects Gaby's jewels to colonial exploitation, of which the wine trade in Algeria is a particularly

Collection Idéale P. S.

66. ALGER — Rue Arabe

Orientalism in popular culture: a 1920s postcard of the Casbah

pointed example: lucrative for the French, it ignored the local culture
which was non-wine drinking.

Colonialism was very prominent in film at the time. North Africa
was by far the most favoured colonial location, and was used in over half
of the 85 or so French films of the 1930s set outside Western countries.
Interestingly, 1931, the year of the Colonial Exhibition, and 1936, the
year *Pépé le Moko* was made, were peak years in French colonial film
production.[44] Colonial cinema was thus a particularly important sub-
genre in the 1930s. The range of directors' names in the following list,
from hallowed auteurs to unknown 'hacks', shows how widespread it
was: Duvivier's *Les Cinq Gentlemen maudits* (1931), Renoir's *Le Bled*
(1932), Edmond T. Gréville's *Princesse Tam-Tam* (1932), G. W. Pabst's
L'Atlantide (1932), Jacques Feyder's *Le Grand jeu* (1933), Marie Epstein
and Jean Benoît-Lévy's *Itto* (1934), Henry Wulschleger's *Sidonie
Panache* (1934), Marcel L'Herbier's *L'Aventurier* (1934), Duvivier's *La
Bandera* (1935), L'Herbier's *Les Hommes nouveaux* (1936), Michel
Bernheim's *Le Roman d'un Spahi* (1936), Fedor Ozep's *Amok* (1933),
Léon Poirier's *L'Appel du silence* (1936), André Hugon's *Sarati le terrible*
(1937), Raymond Rouleau's *Le Messager* (1937), Pierre Colombier's *Un
de la légion* (1937), Chenal's *La Maison du Maltais* (1938). This list is far
from exhaustive. To be sure, these films addressed colonialism in very
different ways, from propaganda (*Les Hommes nouveaux*) to romantic
melodrama (*Le Grand jeu*). In this spectrum, *Pépé le Moko* is not an
avowedly political text; it does not depict or advocate territorial conquest,
unlike, say, *Les Hommes nouveaux*. As François Ramirez and Christian
Rolot argue, it is less overtly racist than many.[45] It inhabits nevertheless
the contradictory space of the colonialist artefact.

The pervasiveness of the colonial genre made its ideology, to some
extent, invisible to contemporaries. Right-wing film historians such as
Maurice Bardèche and Robert Brasillach criticised *Pépé le Moko*'s
celebration of crime, not its colonialism. More surprisingly, communist
historian Georges Sadoul, who in 1931 signed a petition urging 'Do not
visit the Colonial Exhibition!',[46] did not object to *Pépé le Moko* on those
grounds either. Since then, many analyses of *Pépé le Moko* (including
those by myself) have noted its exoticism and racism, but moved on to
concentrate on other issues. More recently, in the wake of Edward Saïd's
Orientalism (1978) and *Culture and Imperialism* (1993), *Pépé le Moko* and
other French colonial films and texts have been vigorously criticised.

Orientalist iconography: Gaby, Pépé and 'Arab' inspector Slimane during Gaby's and Pépé's first meeting

56   Orientalist iconography: Gaby and Pépé with an (uncredited) waitress at café Ali Baba (Carlos in the background)

There is little room for disagreement on the fact that *Pépé le Moko* is steeped in colonialist culture and ideology. Accordingly my aim here is not to 'whitewash' the film, nor to condemn it. Simply, we will examine how the film negotiates its colonial setting within the French populist tradition, especially considering the presence of Jean Gabin, a star positioned to an unusual degree as a national icon.

2. Where are we?

Gaby's friends are designated by the film as caricatural French tourists abroad. Bad-tempered Maxime complains about the heat, Mlle Berthier finds the sun 'so sad', and comic Gravère exclaims, 'I love travel because I always imagine I am somewhere else: in Corsica I thought I was in Turkey, here I am in China.' As if to confirm his vision, the café in which he and his group meet Pépé is called Ali Baba, evoking the Arabia of *A Thousand and One Nights*. Gravère's joke reveals the ambivalent place occupied by Algeria in the French imaginary: so close, yet so far. Ashelbé's book is more brutally explicit. In it, Gaby's companion says: 'Algeria is sufficiently African to give the inhabitants of the Marne [the champagne-growing area] the impression of a faraway location, and close enough to France to go there for prospection without spending too much.'[47] Algiers was the most 'Frenchified' colonial capital, with modern quarters built in the style of late nineteenth-century French provincial architecture. It was seen as an extension of Marseilles, the two cities sharing a number of features. Indeed, in the book Gaby and the visitors express disappointment at its modernity.

Taking its cue from them, the film does not dwell on the modern city. Apart from the harbour views at the end, the scenes at the Hotel Aletti and the police headquarters are mostly indoor locations with nominal signs of exoticism (for example, shadows of palm trees) rather than explicit anchorage. They also avoid showing the outside architecture of the buildings, and the opening montage of the Casbah is not matched by any similar documentary view of the modern quarters. Nevertheless, in the harbour scenes, the straight lines of the ship company shopfront, the views of busy people in Western clothing, and the large quantity of sky serve to enhance the difference with the cramped and dark space of the Casbah, inhabited by people crouching in unfamiliar, non-Western ways, standing in doorways, sitting in courtyards, scurrying around the streets. This spatial configuration embodies the film's key theme of confinement and escape, and conforms to the dominant representation of Algiers in the cinema, before and since.[48] It also prefigures Frantz Fanon's description of the divided colonial city: 'The settler's town is a strongly built town, all made of stone and steel. It is a brightly lit town. [...] The native town is a crouching village, a town on its knees, a town wallowing in the mire. It is a town of niggers and dirty Arabs.'[49] The Casbah in the film reproduces a set of iconographic motifs well in place in the popular imagery of the early twentieth century, especially postcards. Picturesquely named streets and alley-ways are non-linear and on a slant, with great emphasis on stairs, capped by arches, over-hanging awnings and vaults, evoking simultaneously the fortress, the maze and the jungle. The Casbah's image of criminality connotes that other notorious French colonial jail, the *bagne* (Devil's Island). The conflation of criminality and colonial spaces was also reinforced by the figure of the légionnaire, prominent in films and songs of the time ('Mon Légionnaire', sung by Marie Dubas and Edith Piaf, was composed by Raymond Asso in 1936). Pépé could be seen as a perversion of the légionnaire, a soldier usually with a criminal past sent to fight in the colonies on behalf of the French.

At the same time, the Casbah looks marvellously attractive, and its visual beauty should not be underestimated in the success of the film; most reviewers drew attention to the beauty and quality of the sets. The beauty of the Casbah sets is also an expression of its erotic appeal. Malek Alloula, in *The Colonial Harem*,[50] demonstrates how postcards sent by French soldiers home in the early part of the century constructed Arab quarters as closed and exotic, but also, importantly, sexually alluring. MacOrlan's novel *Quartier Réservé* (1932), set in the 'red light' district of Casablanca, similarly describes the native quarter as exuding 'feminine and criminal odours'.[51] Ashelbé and Duvivier's Casbah is also feminine and sexual. It is a chaotic space which, the montage commentary says, includes 'all races, all women'. 'All women', as already noted, means prostitutes. 'All races' is revealing of how exoticism erases cultural specificity. The montage commentary details the different 'races' inhabiting the Casbah and points out its overcrowding ('40,000 where there should be 10,000'). Many groups are named: Kabyles, Chinese, gypsies, *Heimatlos* (stateless), Slavs, Maltese, Blacks, Sicilians, Spaniards, except, extraordinarily, Arabs. The erasure of the name

'Arab' from the commentary continues throughout the film, where as characters they are marginalised or disparaged. Few are given close-ups, and when they are, these shots emphasise either their exotic difference (the young Arab woman) or their negative character (L'Arbi in the scene of his punishment).

It has been argued that the choice of place Blanche as a meeting point for Gaby and Pépé is racist.[52] While the name may seem ironic under the circumstances, the historical specificity of that location should be kept in mind. The geographical reality and cultural identity of place Blanche are more significant to its choice than the metaphorical readings of the word 'white'. Both the place Blanche itself and Fréhel's song (discussed in Chapter 1), in which it figures prominently, predate the film. Other decisions in the film's casting, costumes and acting, on the other hand, are unambiguously racist. Just as Arabs are erased from the list of ethnic groups in the Casbah, their voices are hardly heard in the rest of the film. Throughout *Pépé le Moko*, one hears mutterings, the 'meaningless', because untranslated, sentences of a beggar, 'gibberish', as Pépé says; the function of the untranslated Arab dialogue, such as it is, is to provide local colour and to enshrine one recognisable word: 'Pépé'. The silencing of Arab voices is particularly acute by contrast with the volubility of the actors speaking Jeanson's sparkling dialogue.

Casting and visual treatment continue this theme. 'Indigenous' characters are played by white actors made up to look darker. Dalio, who plays L'Arbi, has a whitened lower lip to enhance the darkness of his face. The same goes for Renée Carl, who plays the Algerian Mère Tarte with a broad Parisian accent. Line Noro, as Inès, is made to look particularly ungainly, with dark make-up, lanky hair, huge ear-rings and a clutter of clashing jewels and clothes, contrasting with the impeccably coiffed and dressed Gaby. Gaby's clothes, with the exception of her grey suit, are made of white, softly shining fabrics and furs which reflect the light (pearls and diamonds adding to the glitter), whereas Inès' only major close-up, described earlier, shows her face covered with dark criss-crossing shadows. Fabrics and lighting make Gaby 'glow', but her complexion remains perfectly matt, as opposed to Inès whose skin shines with sweat; similarly, the young Arab woman who shelters Gaby, though more glamorously presented and lit than Inès, turns a shiny face to the camera next to Gaby's matt complexion. Sweating, associated with

60   Lighting, whiteness and Orientalism: glowing *Parisienne* Gaby (top) and brooding gipsy Inès (bottom)

'natives', is further conflated with treachery in the character of Régis, a hybrid between Charpin's Marseillais identity and 'Arabicity' through his clothes, especially his headgear.

Before *Pépé le Moko*, Lucas Gridoux, an actor of Jewish-Romanian origins, had been confined to small roles, usually of traitors (he played Judas in Duvivier's *Golgotha*). But while Slimane remains his most important part, his characterisation is nevertheless racist. The decision to make him look unsympathetic was conscious on the film-makers' part: cinematographer Jules Kruger reportedly complained that Gridoux was too handsome and relocated spotlights, 'so that Inspector Slimane would not appear too seductive'.[53] Slimane enters the fiction in the police headquarters as the word 'spy' is uttered by one of the inspectors; he is promptly called 'lazy', thus combining two Arab stereotypes, lazy and devious. (Later, Pépé calls him a *faux-jeton*, a hypocrite. We may note in this respect that Inès betrays Pépé to the police, while Gaby, as she says, 'always sticks to her promises'; she fails him only because she is given false information.) Slimane is frequently framed in profile, on the edge of the frame, his back and head bent, his expression a mixture of ingratiating smile and suspicion. As the character who technically brings about Pépé's downfall by introducing Gaby to him and planning and conducting his capture, Slimane is key to the narrative of *Pépé le Moko*. However, his visual treatment described above, his lower status as a performer and the weight of Gabin as a star, and the fact that Pépé's trajectory is self-determined (by committing suicide, he robs Slimane of his victory), all go towards undermining Slimane's structural importance and explaining his relatively marginal place on the credits of the film.[54]

Altogether, then, the Casbah conforms to its stereotype, as described by Fanon as 'a place of ill fame, peopled by men of evil repute'. Mention is made of 'vermin', of 'bad smells'. Bad characters are Arabs (Slimane, L'Arbi) or those made Arab-like (Régis); they are marginalised and sometimes rendered ugly by framing and lighting. 'Good' characters, enhanced by the camera, are French and have old-fashioned French names: Grand Père, Pierrot, Gaby and, of course, Pépé. Ultimately, the 'sordidness' of the Casbah and its native or near-native inhabitants acts as a foil to the glowing romantic couple formed by Pépé–Gabin and Gaby–Balin – so glamorous that it was immediately recast, the same year, in Jean Grémillon's *Gueule d'amour*. Yet the French characters, an assembly of marginals, hoodlums and prostitutes, are hardly paragons of virtue.

3. Populism and orientalism: a national icon in the Casbah

Pépé le Moko was shot during the Left-centrist alliance of the Popular Front, which had come to power in June 1936. Duvivier and Gabin had just made *La Belle équipe*, a film ostensibly atuned to the issues of that time, though Duvivier disclaimed having made a political film. In *La Belle équipe* Gabin and his friends are Parisian workers who jointly win the lottery and decide to pool their resources; they form a kind of cooperative and restore a riverside inn, a *guinguette* where, in the spirit of the newly won paid holidays, people flock at the weekend. Internal tensions and the machinations of a scheming woman (Viviane Romance) sabotage the enterprise until only Jean (Gabin) and his friend Charles (Vanel) are left, and Jean kills Charles. A preview audience rejected that ending, and Duvivier shot an upbeat version in which Jean and Charles send the woman packing and remain friends. Despite this change of ending, *La Belle équipe* was not a great success. It is tempting to see the much more popular *Pépé le Moko* as a successfully escapist film which turns its back on the contemporary political situation, investing instead in the double exoticism of the Hollywood-style gangster and of the Casbah. But *Pépé le Moko* is a film of its time, just as much as *La Belle équipe*. The importance of the colonial sub-genre shows how the preoccupation with the colonies percolated down to popular cinema. Concurrently, *Pépé le Moko* is defined by two counter-trends concerned with definitions of a national culture, apparently disconnected from the colonial setting and ideology. One is that *Pépé le Moko* is shot through with a populist culture which celebrates Paris and a particular fringe of its population. And the other is that Jean Gabin's image as a star was closely associated with a notion of 'authentic' Frenchness.

Yet, ironically, the star persona of Gabin as 'ideal Frenchman' was largely forged in colonial spaces. In *La Bandera*, he is a criminal and a sympathetic working-class hero, but this identity is bound up with racial superiority. Under the 'clean slate' policy of the Foreign Legion, his fight against Arab 'rebels' determines his heroic status as Frenchman by erasing his earlier, socially anchored, French crime. His class identity is elevated to the status of a national one thanks to the colonial context (in 1943, Duvivier and Gabin reprised a similar story in *The Impostor*, but this time the villains were the Germans). *Pépé le Moko* continues the work of *La Bandera* in using exotic and colonialist depictions to shore up the national identity and glamour of its hero. The audience, like him, is transplanted to the exotic space, in which he is the main point of identification. This is a major difference with Ashelbé's book, which uses the character of Carlo as narrator in the early part of the novel and presents Pépé to the reader as a curious and exotic character himself, and also with the remakes of the film, which merge French with North African exoticism (see Chapter 4). In *Pépé le Moko*, identification with Pépé is totally overdetermined. It is prepared by the pre-existing image of the star, reinforced by the relegation of Carlos to a marginal figure, and compounded by the multiplication of white, gleaming ties and scarves and the luminous enhancement of his face which make him a desirable, glamorous, white figure.

Pépé's sexual aura marks him out. He is 'loved by all women' ('There will be 3,000 widows at his funeral'), while the native or semi-native men who surround him – Régis, L'Arbi, Slimane – have no sexuality and are consistently humiliated by him. Slimane in particular is the butt of covert homophobic jibes, as Pépé mockingly accuses him of wearing mascara and having his hair permed. The insistence on Gabin as sexually and racially superior to Slimane, like their vows of mutual hostility, is part of the film's colonialist stance since it suggests a white supremacist masculinity. But it can also be read against the grain as covering anxieties about masculine and racial identity. For Pépé's relation to the Casbah is itself ambivalent. It protects and emprisons him. He is both *of* the Casbah and alien to it. The *caïd des caïds*, he dominates it in a way which can be compared to the common representation in the films of the time of the classic virile colonialist who dominates the 'feminised' colonial space.[55] At the same time, though, the strong eroticisation of the Casbah, its feminine identity, imprison him and 'feminise' him too. His struggle to free himself of this literally and metaphorically cloying feminine and colonial environment, is, from the beginning, a struggle towards death.

For the spectator of 1937, there was an added layer of meaning to this tale, which complicates a simple racial dichotomy, and that is the class dimension. Popular colonial culture addressed a working-class audience. In many films, the white hero who dies at the hand of the native 'rebels', in the heat, the sun, and the wind is a working-class man.

In two popular songs of the time, Piaf's 'Mon Légionnaire' and Fréhel's 'Derrière la clique', the French heroes are lads from Pantin and Belleville, dying in 'the wretched sirocco wind', while singing 'Pan-pan L'Arbi!' ('Kill the Arab'). *La Bandera* and *Sidonie Panache*, like *Pépé le Moko* too, construct a class-inflected national identity mapped over the colonial experience. The law in *Pépé le Moko* is unambiguously identified with the bourgeoisie: Slimane, the lackey of the French police, enlists Maxime's help in luring Pépé out of the Casbah. *Pépé le Moko* replicates in a colonial context the dilemma of working-class masculinity addressed in other Gabin films: he may be the *caïd* of his little world, but outside he is nothing. Contained and aestheticised in the *ʒone*, in the Casbah or in Montmartre, the *apache* is celebrated by populist fiction, as long as he does not step beyond the limits of his prescribed terrain. While Algiers' Casbah was recreated in the Parisian suburbs at Joinville, a whole *quartier* of Paris, namely Montmartre and Pigalle, travelled through the Gabin character to the Casbah of *Pépé le Moko*. This association is suggested on a literal level by the hilly relief, narrow streets and size of both areas, but more powerfully on a metaphorical level by the double association with sexuality and crime: it is in Montmartre '*du plaisir et du crime*', in Louis Chevalier's phrase,[56] that the *apache* finds his 'natural' habitat. The rich bourgeois, *especially* at the time of the Popular Front, will see to it that he remains there. Although Gaby regrets not seeing Pépé again, she does stay with Maxime, his champagne and the jewels. Like the spectator's, her gaze at the end of the film combines Pépé and the Casbah in a dreamy erotic fantasy which distances the working-class hero and keeps him in his place.

Pépé le Moko, in common with the best French populist films of the 1930s, offers a double position to its spectators, aligning them both with the bourgeois (and bourgeoises) who enjoy the rough erotic appeal of the *apache*, and with the working-class spectators who empathise with him. *Pépé le Moko*, I believe, ultimately sides with the working-class hero, as the last image returns us to what Gaby and her friends cannot see, Pépé's suicide and *his* vision, through the closed gates of the harbour, of his irretrievably lost hopes which the ship takes away. The colonial setting serves to enable this 'Franco-French' drama to take place and throw into relief the class identity of those made to serve, often against their will, the bourgeois state's colonial imperatives. In this tale of two cities, where the exotic fantasy of Algiers dominates the image

The final separation: Top: Gaby on the ship; middle: Pépé behind the gates, about to commit suicide; bottom: the Ville d'Oran sails towards France while the nostalgic fantasy of Paris dominates the soundtrack, the French working-class hero is, in both places, culturally dominant but politically subaltern.

4

THE OTHER PÉPÉS

In the last twenty years, we have become familiar with American remakes of French films, with such high-profile cases as *Le Retour de Martin Guerre (Sommersby)*, *Nikita (The Assassin)*, *La Totale (True Lies)* and *Les Diaboliques (Diabolique)*. But the phenomenon goes further back than the last two decades. Although *Algiers*, the 1938 remake of *Pépé le Moko*, was not the first American remake of a French film, it was a well-publicised instance which prompted the kind of criticism which would be heard through the 1980s and 1990s. First, that remakes are commercially detrimental to the French film industry; P. A. Harlé, editor of the trade magazine *La Cinématographie française*, summed up the French position: 'The sale of the story of a French film can ruin its career abroad. It is a new method. Instead of selling *Pépé le Moko* to America, its subject was sold. Not only will the Gabin film not be shown on the other side of the Atlantic, but even in French-speaking countries, *Algiers*, with Charles Boyer in the Gabin part, will be shown instead of the French original!'[57] Secondly, remakes are seen as automatically inferior to their 'original'. If the industry's point is unarguably true, the aesthetic one is dubious as a generalisation. But the fact remains that, by virtue of being similar yet different, remakes can throw light on the specificity of the source film – and maybe of French film in general. With this in mind, I will briefly analyse *Pépé le Moko*'s two remakes, *Algiers* and *Casbah*. I will also comment on the idiosyncratic *Totó le Mokó* and on distant derivations of the character of Pépé in Zero Mostel's character in *Dubarry Was a Lady* and in the cartoon series *Pepe le Pew*.

Algiers was directed by John Cromwell in 1938, with Charles Boyer as Pépé and Hedy Lamarr as Gaby, Sigrid Gurie as Inès and Joseph Calleia as Slimane. *Algiers* was a high-profile and successful film, in turn influencing other American derivations of *Pépé le Moko*. Although the success of *Pépé le Moko* was responsible for Duvivier's and Mireille Balin's invitation to Hollywood, and there was talk of Duvivier directing the remake himself, Cromwell shot it, reportedly with a copy of Duvivier's film on the moviola during the shoot. Similarities between the two films are indeed striking. Except for the ending, *Algiers* follows the same narrative line as *Pépé le Moko* and foregrounds the same key scenes, including those not in the book, such as the exchange of Parisian street names, and Pépé's song (though Tania's song is missing). Dialogue, setting, characters' hairstyle and clothing, are similar. Documentary shots from Duvivier's opening montage are re-used, as well as passages of music by Scotto and Yguerbouchen.

In many ways, then, *Algiers* is the replica of *Pépé le Moko* it claimed to be. But on closer inspection, divergences are equally striking and instructive. *Algiers* is definitely less noir than *Pépé le Moko*. More scenes are shot with high-key lighting and if chiaroscuro is used – for instance, when Aïcha fetches Pépé, and at the beginning of Régis' interrogation – the contrast is softer. Décor establishes exoticism, but is less enclosing than in *Pépé le Moko*: streets are wider, there are fewer arches and overhanging elements of architecture. As Pépé and Slimane walk the streets, the décor recedes further in the background, giving more prominence to the actors. Inès' flat looks more Western (with square windows and pieces of Western-looking furniture). The back room at L'Algérien is larger and the shot of Inès looking through the lacy curtain is less tightly framed. Pépé's wild outburst after Pierrot's death and his interrogation of L'Arbi lack the tension of the French film. As is often the case in Hollywood remakes of French films, plot details are made visually or verbally more explicit. For instance, just after the credits a text printed over a shot of the harbour describes the Casbah, duplicating the dialogue in the following scene. When Gaby tells Slimane that policemen are stupid (not knowing he is one of them), she is immediately corrected instead of being left to discover his identity later by herself as in *Pépé le Moko*. Again as in many other remakes, action opportunities are stepped up, in this case in the scene of the police raid. Unlike in the French film, where they are content to crawl through the streets and fire a few ineffectual shots, police in *Algiers* ram through a door, stereotypically burst into a room, and a little later chase the gangsters across terraces and rooftops. Finally, sexuality and crime have been 'cleaned up'. The theme of prostitution is eliminated: images of prostitutes in the Casbah montage are virtually eradicated, and Gaby and Maxime are engaged to be married. The relationship between Pépé and Inès is more affectionate and there is no mention of Carlos's brutality to Tania. The most noticeable change is in the ending. Pépé is taken, handcuffed, behind the harbour railings, but as he starts walking back towards the departing ship he is shot by one of the policemen. As Slimane bends over him and (redundantly) says, 'I'm sorry, Pépé, he thought you were going to escape,' Pépé replies before dying, 'So I have, my friend.' *Algiers* thus fits the Hays code moral scheme of crime and punishment.

In the same way that the rougher, darker and amoral mood of *Pépé le Moko* is epitomised by Gabin, so the lighter, more conventional tone of *Algiers* is well served by Boyer. A highbrow actor in the bourgeois theatrical tradition, with a refined voice and smooth facial features, Boyer tones Pépé down. Notwithstanding his talent, Boyer remains an actor impersonating a character, where Gabin exudes a sense of authenticity. However, if Boyer was dubbed 'Pépé le Monsieur' in France, internationally he provided a readily acceptable version of Frenchness or Europeanness, honed in his earlier Hollywood films such as *Caravan* (1934), *The Garden of Allah* (1936) and *Conquest* (1936). The key to Boyer's success as Pépé for international audiences was his condensation of the double exoticism of North Africa and France – whereas Gabin embodied a sharp distinction between the two.

Boyer's fame as Pépé was comically acknowledged by Zero Mostel in his Hollywood debut in the Arthur Freed musical *Dubarry Was a Lady* (1943, starring Lucille Ball, Gene Kelly and Red Skelton, directed by Roy del Ruth). Mostel, like the other characters in the film, plays a dual role, a performer in a Broadway cabaret and a 'period' character in a dream sequence set at the time of Louis XV. It is in the former role, as 'Rami the Swami', that early in the film he performs a parody of Boyer to a female customer, putting on Boyer's hairstyle, seducer's gaze and French accent, especially his pronunciation of 'Cas-baaah'. Mostel's number is inserted as a performance within a performance, in the stand-up comic tradition the actor came from. The only connection to the rest of the film, apart from the French setting of the period story, is Mostel's 'oriental' costume, condensing again Frenchness and orientalism.

Two years later, in 1945, another comic derivation of Boyer's Pépé came in the shape of a Warner Bros.' cartoon character, *Pepe le Pew*

Three Pépés. Top: *Pépé le Moko* (1937): Gabin as Pépé with (left to right) Max, Slimane
and Jimmy; middle: *Algiers* (1938): Charles Boyer (left) as Pépé, with Joseph Calleia as
Slimane; bottom: *Casbah* (1948): Tony Martin as Pépé

(sometimes spelt Pepé), created by Chuck Jones. Although Pepe le Pew is generally regarded as inferior to other, more famous, Jones creations such as the Road Runner, it nevertheless earned him an Oscar, awarded to *For Scent-imental Reasons* (1951). Apart from *Cats-bah* (1954), most of the Pepe le Pew cartoons have no connection with the location or story of *Pépé le Moko*. They refer instead to the stereotypical Frenchness of Boyer and by extension all Frenchmen, by parodying Boyer's (and, reputedly, Maurice Chevalier's) accent and his romantic persona, and setting many of the stories in France: for instance, at the Louvre museum in *Louvre Come Back to Me*, or in the French Alps for *Two Scent's Worth*. As the name suggests, Pepe le Pew is a foul-smelling black and white skunk who relentlessly pursues female cats who accidentally have a white stripe painted on their back (thus leading Pepe to think they are female skunks), but is invariably betrayed by his smell to which many of the titles allude: *Two Scent's Worth*, *Odor of the Day*, etc. Even taking into account Jones's customary caustic humour and his interesting statement that Pepe represented 'what I wanted to be, and what I think every man would like to be: irresistible, at least in one's own eyes',[58] this American view of Frenchness is distinctly unflattering. French male seduction translates as harassment and ridiculous pretence. The smell conflates, on a literal level, popular American views of French 'garlic eating' habits and 'primitive' sanitation – views that were possibly reinforced at the time, by returning GIs – with, on a metaphorical level, their supposed excessive sexuality (Jones commented that Pepe le Pew was the only cartoon character overtly interested in sex),[59] all compounded with the 'odours' associated with the Casbah in the various versions of *Pépé le Moko*.

A more flattering, if also stereotypical view of Frenchness is presented in *Casbah*, a musical directed by John Berry in 1948, with Tony Martin as Pépé, Marta Toren as Gaby, Yvonne De Carlo as Inès and Peter Lorre as Slimane. *Casbah* credits Ashelbé's novel as its source and a trace of this can be found in the larger role given to Carlo(s). However, the Marseilles episode is left out and in other ways, too, *Casbah* is predicated on the preceding films rather than the book. For instance, the scene of Pépé singing and the women of the Casbah listening to him echoes the same scene (not in the book) from *Pépé le Moko* and *Algiers*. As a musical *Casbah* develops different aesthetic strategies from the other two films, using the romantic narrative as a peg for sentimental crooner Tony

Martin, and an entirely different musical score. Pépé's and Gaby's romantic reunion is a serenade by Pépé on the Casbah terraces. Pépé and Gaby's fox-trot is much extended and there are scenes featuring Katherine Dunham's black dancers. *Casbah*'s softer, more sentimental approach to the story, like that of *Algiers*, also draws it towards romance; many contemporary reviewers of both *Casbah* and *Algiers* noted the films' special appeal to women.

Casbah acknowledges the ten-year gap with the two preceding films. The Casbah itself is more distanced, its exoticism more knowing, through the device of a tourist guide 'explaining' it to a group of tourists. Allusions to *Casablanca* (1943), which itself references *Pépé le Moko*,[60] are also clearly signalled. Apart from the similarity in titles, *Casbah* alludes to the Curtiz film in three obvious ways. First, the Casbah décor features several prominent posters bearing the name 'Vichy'. Secondly, Peter Lorre (as Slimane) brilliantly reprises his 'blandly bemused sleuthing'[61] persona (not confined to that film, but made famous largely thanks to it). Finally, the ending substitutes the airport to the harbour: Pépé is shot by the police as Gaby's aeroplane takes off.

Totó le Mokó was directed in 1949 by Carlo Ludovico Bragaglia, one of Totó's regular directors, while the star was at the height of his popularity. It is tailored to his image and talent, and comedy stems from the gap between the familiar Totó and the new character, in this case Pépé, a gap illustrated by the title of the film. Totó thus is a Naples street musician summoned to Algiers upon the death of his famous relative Pépé. Playing on the double meaning of the Italian word 'banda' (musical band and gang), the film shows Totó believing that Pépé's friends form a musical band of which they want him to be the leader – until their first 'performance' at the Grand Hotel, where they get machine-guns out of their cases instead of instruments. From weakling, Totó turns into virile gang leader, thanks to a magic hair lotion given to him by Pépé's ex-girl friend (the Inès character). This enables him also to seduce a beautiful blonde (the Gaby character). In the most extraordinary scene of the film, Totó, in pin-stripe suit, black shirt and white tie, postures as tough gangster for the assembled company and performs a comic and ludicrously violent *apache* dance which includes him knocking his female partner's head on a wooden banister in step with the music. *Totó le Mokó* conflates the *apache* stereotype with Totó's persona, capitalising on his 'disjointed physique which he used like a surreal puppet', in Goffredo Fofi's excellent definition.[62] Shortly after, the 'real' Pépé, who is not dead after all, comes back, but the blundering Totó gets the better of him despite Inès' recourse to a witch, is praised for his capture of the notorious criminal and returns to Naples to become a famous orchestra conductor. The Casbah of *Totó le Mokó* is, like that of *Algiers* and *Casbah*, more of a distant background than that of *Pépé le Moko*. As in the other remakes too, French and North African exoticisms merge in an address to a non-French audience: *apache*-looking characters wearing cloth caps mingle with figures in Arab dress in the streets of the Casbah. The homogenising effect is compounded by the fact that all the characters speak Italian (peppered with a few French expressions).

Unsurprisingly, then, the film is put to the service of Totó's aggressive and unconventional persona, 'perpetually hungry for food, for sex, for a place in the sun', to quote Fofi again. In this respect only, Totó's version of Pépé gets close to some aspects of the character in the book, a brutal ruffian who demands, and obtains, immediate sexual satisfaction with Gaby. The victory of the inept character over strong and glamorous superiors belongs to the comic tradition, that of Totó and others. Otherwise, the film borrows from other remakes. For instance, the scene of Totó/Pépé's arrest in the Casbah and release as various Casbah inhabitants eliminate policemen one after the other is only seen in *Casbah*, whereas it does not figure in either book or film of *Pépé le Moko* (or in *Algiers*).

Ultimately, each of these filmic manifestations of 'Pépé le Moko' uses plot elements and visual motifs to its own ends, whether it is romantic melodrama, musical, comedy or cartoon. But in their varied ways, these films speak of a lasting fascination with *Pépé le Moko* the film and with Pépé the character, through imitation or counterpoint. They send us back to Duvivier's film and to Gabin's interpretation.

CONCLUSION

Pépé's numerous manifestations speak of his enduring evocative power, far beyond the cheap gangster created by Ashelbé. He is a contradictory yet powerful figure of identification, the outsider who belongs, the loner who sums up an ideal community, corresponding to an idealised sense of national character, typical of the French cinema of the 1930s. His name, which ties the mundane 'Pépé' to the flavourful 'Moko', gives a clue to his dual appeal. Various interpretations of the name 'Moko' have been offered: 'from Marseilles' or the midi generally or from Moka, a port in Arabia from which the name of mocha coffee is derived, are the most common. Duvivier for his part claims that it means 'tough guy' in Toulon slang.[63] Whatever, the connotations are Mediterranean, dark and flamboyant, adding an alluring layer of exoticism to Gabin's strongly anchored Parisian image, another imaginary link between France and North Africa.

Pépé le Moko is the perfect blend of crime and romance, of sleaze and poetry, which explains how the film could have given rise to remakes that range from romantic woman's melodrama (*Algiers, Casbah*) to robust comedy (*Totó le Mokó*). *Pépé le Moko*'s direct heirs are the ageing gangsters of the 1950s, especially Max le menteur of *Touchez pas au grisbi* (played by an ageing Gabin) and Bob of *Bob le flambeur*. Further afield, in his mixture of tough guy and romantic, Pépé is the ancestor of Michel Poiccard (Jean-Paul Belmondo) in *A bout de souffle* (1959) and of the elegant hero of *Le Samouraï*, played by Alain Delon. In this respect, Pépé cannot be separated from Gabin. The pre-war mythology of the star as tragic working-class hero gave depth and humanity to the small-time gangster while the Hollywood-inspired visual glamour of the mobster reflected back on Gabin's proletarian image. If, to quote Graham Greene again, *Pépé le Moko* 'succeeded so admirably in raising the thriller to a poetic level',[64] it is thus in large measure thanks to its star. But it is also due to the perfection of the ensemble work of its décor, cast, dialogue, music and camerawork and of its supremely assured direction. *Pépé le Moko* condenses a whole era of French film-making. As such, it is both absolutely dated and perfectly ageless. In short, a classic.

NOTES

. . . .

1 Henri La Barthe wrote other thrillers under the name of Ashelbé and film scripts. In particular, his *Dédée d'Anvers* was adapted by Yves Allégret in 1948, starring Simone Signoret. In the 1930s his most famous book, apart from *Pépé le Moko*, was *Les Curieuses enquêtes de M. Petivillain détective* (1930).

2 *Pépé le Moko* was seventh at the French box-office in a particularly strong year for French cinema. It exported very successfully, except in the US, where its release was held until the release of the remake *Algiers*.

3 Jean Cocteau, quoted in Nicole and Alain Lacombe, *Fréhel* (Paris: Pierre Belfond, 1990), p. 219. Graham Greene, *The Spectator*, April 1937, in John Russell Taylor (ed.), *The Pleasure Dome: Graham Greene, The Collected Film Criticism 1935–40* (Oxford: Oxford University Press, 1980), p. 144.

4 Nino Frank, 'A la Casbah d'Alger, *Pépé le Moko*', *Pour Vous*, no. 429, 4 February 1937.

5 On *Pépé le Moko*, colonialism and orientalism, see Janice Morgan, 'In the Labyrinth: Masculine Subjectivity, Expatria-tion and Colonialism in *Pépé le Moko*', in Matthew Bernstein and Gaylyn Studlar (eds), *Visions of the East, Orientalism in Film* (London: I. B. Tauris Publishers, 1997), pp. 253–68; Martin O'Shaughnessy, '*Pépé le Moko* or the Impossibility of Being French in the 1930s', *French Cultural Studies*, vol. 7, 1996, pp. 247–58; Deborah Linderman, paper on *Pépé le Moko* delivered at *Society for Cinema Studies*, May 1992, unpublished.

6 T. S. Eliot, *What Is A Classic?* (London: Faber and Faber, 1945), p. 16.

7 Duvivier directed *Le Petit monde de Don Camillo* in 1952 and *Le Retour de Don Camillo* in 1953, both starring Fernandel and Gino Cervi; the success of the series was such that six films altogether were made, although Duvivier gave up directing them after the first two.

8 See Colin Crisp, *The Classic French Cinema, 1930–1960* (Bloomington: Indiana University Press, 1993).

9 King Vidor, quoted in Raymond Chirat, *Julien Duvivier* (Lyon: Premier Plan, 1968), p. 16.

10 Duvivier was one of the administrators of the film-makers' union 'Syndicat des Chefs Cinéastes Français', together with Jean Renoir and André Berthomieu (see Crisp, *The Classic French Cinema*, p. 198).

11 Interview with Julien Duvivier, *Cinémonde*, 15 September 1959, pp. 14–16.

12 On Poetic Realism, see Dudley Andrew, *Mists of Regret: Culture and Sensibility in Classic French Film* (Princeton: Princeton University Press, 1995).

13 See Ginette Vincendeau, 'Noir is also a French Word', in Ian Cameron (ed.), *The Movie Book of Film Noir* (London: Studio Vista, 1992), pp. 39–58, and Charles O'Brien, 'Film Noir in France: Before the Liberation', *Iris*, no. 21, Spring 1996, pp. 7–20.

14 Interview with Julien Duvivier, *Cinémonde*.

15 See Michel Marie, '*Pépé le Moko*: La Valse des caméras', in *L'Avant-scène du cinéma*, 1 June 1981, pp. 6–7.

16 Italo Calvino, 'Autobiographie d'un spectateur', *Positif, no.* 181, May 1975, quoted in Dudley Andrew, *Mists of Regret*, p. 188

17 'Quand la Casbah d'Alger s'installe à Joinville', *Cinémonde*, 17 December 1936; Duvivier reports that rain in Algiers prevented more lengthy shooting, in 'A Alger la blanche, quand Duvivier tournait "Pépé le Moko"', *Ciné-Miroir*, 7 May 1937, p. 310.

18 Léon Barsacq, *Le Décor au cinéma* (Paris: Cinéma Club Seghers, 1970), p. 165.

19 For details of comparative stylistic practices in the French and American cinema, see Barry Salt, *Film Style & Technology: History & Analysis* (London: Starword, 1983), and Colin Crisp, *The Classic French Cinema*.

20 Cocteau, in Lacombe, *Fréhel*. On Fréhel, see also Ginette Vincendeau, 'The Mise-en-scène of Suffering: French Realist Women Singers', *New Formations*, vol. l, no. 3, December 1987, pp. 107–128.

21 Raymond Chirat and Olivier Barrot, *Les Excentriques du cinéma français (1929–1958)* (Paris: Henri Veyrier, 1983).

22 Richard Dyer, *Stars* (London: BFI, 1979).

23 Marcel Carné, 'Jean Gabin, un chic type', *Cinemagazine*, Janvier 33.

24 A rare exception to the general pattern governing the lighting of heterosexual couples analysed by Richard Dyer in *White* (London: Routledge, 1997).

25 The expression *policier* (in slang, *polar*) has come to cover most forms of French crime literature and film, whether oriented towards detection, crime or police activities.

26 Georges Sadoul, *Dictionnaire des Films*, Nouvelle Edition Microcosme (Paris: Microcosme/Seuil, 1981), p. 238. Many reviewers and commentators shared Sadoul's view.

27 Graham Greene, *The Pleasure Dome*.

28 Julien Duvivier, interview in *Cinémonde*.

29 Louis Chevalier, *Classes Laborieuses et classes dangereuses* (Paris: Plon, 1958).

30 Gilbert Salachas et Séeberger frères, *Le Paris d'Hollywood, Sur un air de réalité* (Paris: Caisse Nationale des Monuments Historique et des Sites, 1994).

31 Quoted in Farid Chenoune, *A History of Men's Fashion* (Paris: Flammarion, 1993), p. 195.

32 Ibid., p. 196.

33 From an interview with Doriane in André Brunelin, *Jean Gabin* (Paris: Editions Robert Laffont, 1988), p. 205.

34 Michèle Morgan, *With Those Eyes, An Autobiography* (London: W. H. Allen), p. 74.

35 Chenoune, *A History of Men's Fashion*, p. 196.

36 Brunelin, *Jean Gabin*, p. 205.

37 For a further development of the male group in *Pépé le Moko*, see Ginette Vincendeau, 'Community, Nostalgia and the Spectacle of Masculinity', *Screen*, vol. 26, no. 6, 1985, pp. 18–38.

38 Maurice Bardèche and Robert Brasillach, *Histoire du cinéma* (London: Allen and Unwin, 1953).

39 Quoted in Charles O'Brien, 'Film Noir in France: Before the Liberation', *Iris*, no. 21, Spring 1996, p. 12.

40 Chirat, *Julien Duvivier*.

41 Détective Ashelbé, *Pépé le Moko* (Paris: Editions A. I. D., 1931), p. 31.

42 Quoted in Charles-Robert Agron, 'L'Exposition coloniale de 1931, Mythe républicain ou mythe impérial', in Pierre Nora (ed.), *Les Lieux de mémoire*, tome I, *La République* (Paris: Gallimard, 1984), p. 572.

43 *L'Illustration*, special issue on L'Exposition coloniale, 1931.

44 Geneviève Nesterenko, 'L'Afrique de l'autre', in Michèle Lagny, Marie-Claire Ropars and Pierre Sorlin, *Générique des années 30* (Vincennes: Presses Universitaires de Vincennes, 1986), p. 127.

45 François Ramirez et Christian Rolot, 'La Casbah des insoumis, Alger dans *Pépé le Moko* de Julien Duvivier', in Naget Khadda et Paul Siblot (eds), *Alger, Une ville et ses discours* (Montpellier: Praxiling, 1996), pp. 379–99.

46 Charles-Robert Agron, 'L'Exposition coloniale de 1931'. Opposition to the Exhibition, prompted in particular by the Surrealists, remained marginal.

47 Ashelbé, *Pépé le Moko*, pp. 91–2.

48 Ramirez et Rolot, 'La Casbah des insoumis'.

49 Frantz Fanon, *The Wretched of the Earth* (Harmondsworth: Penguin, 1967), p. 30.

50 Malek Alloula, *The Colonial Harem* (Manchester: Manchester University Press, 1986).

51 Pierre MacOrlan, *Quartier réservé*, p. 52.

52 Deborah Linderman, unpublished paper.

53 Françoise Holbane, 'Le vrai visage de Lucas Gridoux', *Ciné-Miroir*, 2 April 1937, p. 222.

54 Lucas Gridoux's marginal place on the credits is noted by Geneviève Nesterenko in Lagny et al., *Générique des années 30*, as typical of the place of non-white characters on the credits of French colonial films of the 1930s. While I agree with this, the case of Gridoux in *Pépé le Moko* is complicated by the status of the performer and the character's place in the mise-en-scène.

55 As analysed by Abdelkader Benali in *L'Espace maghrébin dans le cinéma colonial français (1919–1939)*, unpublished thesis, Université de Paris X-Nanterre, 1997.

56 Louis Chevalier, *Montmartre du plaisir et du crime* (Paris: Robert Laffont, 1980).

57 *La Cinématographie française*, 23 September 1938.

58 Interview with Chuck Jones, *Film Comment*, vol. 11, no. 1, Jan–Feb 1975.
59 Ibid.
60 As Umberto Eco argues in 'Casablanca: Cult Movies and Intertextual Collage', in *Faith in Fakes* (London: Secker and Warburg, 1986), pp. 197–211.
61 *Today's Cinema*, 25 January 1949.
62 Goffredo Fofi, 'Totó', in Ginette Vincendeau (ed.), *Encyclopedia of European Cinema* (London: BFI/Cassell, 1995), p. 426.

63 André Sarrouy, 'Julien Duvivier est passé à Alger pour repérer les extérieurs de "Pépé le Moko"', *Pour Vous*, 7 May 1936. It is alleged (though I found no confirmation of this) that Ashelbé's novel was based on a real criminal from the midi, hence the name of the character.
64 Graham Greene, *The Pleasure Dome*.

CREDITS

· ·

Pépé Le Moko

France
1937

Production Comapny
Paris-Films-Productions
Production Manager
A. Gargour
Director
Julien Duvivier
Assistant Director
Robert Vernay
Scenario
Detective Ashelbé, Julien
Duvivier
Adaptation
Jacques Constant
Based on the novel by
Detective Ashelbé
Dialogue
Henri Jeanson
Directors of Photography
Jules Kruger, Marc Fossard
Editor
Marguerite Beaugé
Art Director
Jacques Krauss
Music
Vincent Scotto, Mohamed
Yguerbouchen
Sound Engineer
Antoine Archaimbaud

Jean Gabin
Pépé le Moko
Gabriel Gabrio
Carlos
Saturnin Fabre
Grand Père
Fernand Charpin
Régis
Lucas Gridoux
Inspector Slimane
Gilbert-Gil
Pierrot
Marcel Dalio
L'Arbi
Charles Granval
Maxime
Gaston Modot
Jimmy
René Bergeron
Meunier
Paul Escoffier
Louvain
Roger Legris
Max
Jean Témerson
Gravère
Robert Ozanne
Gendron
Philippe Richard
Janvier
Georges Péclet
Barsac
Mireille Balin
Gaby
Line Noro
Inès
Fréhel
Tania
Olga Lord
Aïcha
Renée Carl
La Mère Tarte
Frank Maurice
police inspector

93 minutes
8,350 feet

Credits compiled by Markku
Salmi.

SELECT BIBLIOGRAPHY

· ·

French cinema in the 1930s

Crisp, Colin, *The Classic French Cinema, 1930–1960* (Bloomington: Indiana University Press, 1993).

Andrew, Dudley, *Mists of Regret: Culture and Sensibility in Classic French Film* (Princeton: Princeton University Press, 1995).

Martin, John W., *The Golden Age of French Cinema* (London: Columbus Books, 1983).

Lagny, Michèle, Marie-Claire Ropars, Pierre Sorlin, *Générique des Années 30* (Vincennes: Presses Universitaires de Vincennes, 1986).

Pépé le Moko

Ashelbé, Détective, *Pépé le Moko* (Paris: Editions A. I. D., 1931).

Viazzi, Glauco (ed.), *Il bandito della Casbah* (Place: Editoriale Domus, 1945).

L'Avant-scène du cinéma, 'Pépé le Moko', 1 June 1981.

Julien Duvivier

Chirat, Raymond, *Julien Duvivier* (Lyon: Premier Plan, 1968).

Leprohon, Pierre, *Julien Duvivier*, *Anthologie du cinéma*, vol. 4, Paris, 1969.

Tassone, Aldo (a cura di), Pierre Billard, Hubert Niogret, *Julien Duvivier*, France Cinéma, Editrice Il Castoro, n.d. [c. 1996].

Jean Gabin

Brunelin, André, *Jean Gabin* (Paris: Editions Robert Laffont, 1987).

Gauteur, Claude et Ginette Vincendeau, *Anatomie d'un mythe: Jean Gabin* (Paris: Editions Nathan Université, 1993).

ALSO PUBLISHED

If you would like further information about future BFI Film Classics or about other books on film, media and popular culture from BFI Publishing, please write to:

**BFI Film Classics
BFI Publishing
21 Stephen Street
London W1P 2LN**

BFI Film Classics '... could scarcely be improved upon ... informative, intelligent, jargon-free companions.'
The Observer

Each book in the BFI Publishing Film Classics series honours a great film from the history of world cinema. With new titles published each year, the series is rapidly building into a collection representing some of the best writing on film. If you would like to receive further information about future Film Classics or about other books on film, media and popular culture from BFI Publishing, please fill in your name and address and return this card to the BFI*.

No stamp is needed if posted in the UK, Channel Islands, or Isle of Man.

NAME

ADDRESS

POSTCODE

*North America: Please return your card to: Indiana University Press, Attn: LPB, 601 N Morton Street, Bloomington, IN 47401-3797

BFI Publishing
21 Stephen Street
FREEPOST 7
LONDON
W1E 4AN